TESTS
to accompany

English 2600
with Writing Applications

A PROGRAMMED COURSE IN
GRAMMAR AND USAGE

Sixth College Edition

Joseph C. Blumenthal

Harcourt Brace College Publishers
Fort Worth Philadelphia San Diego New York Orlando Austin San Antonio
Toronto Montreal London Sydney Tokyo

Copyright © 1989, 1981, 1973, 1969, 1962, 1960 by
Harcourt Brace & Company
Copyright renewed 1962, 1960 by Margaret W. Blumenthal

All rights reserved. No part of this publication may be reproduced or transmitted in
any form or by any means, electronic or mechanical, including photocopy, recording,
or any information storage and retrieval system, without permission in writing from
the publisher.

Although for mechanical reasons all pages of this publication are perforated, only
those pages imprinted with a Harcourt Brace & Company copyright notice are
intended for removal.

Requests for permission to make copies of any part of the work should be mailed to:
Permissions Department, Harcourt Brace & Company, 8th Floor, Orlando, Florida
32887.

ISBN: 0-15-500864-1

Printed in the United States of America

3 4 5 6 7 8 9 0 1 2   095   9 8 7 6 5 4 3 2 1

A NOTE TO THE INSTRUCTOR

To ensure that the tests in this book really serve to measure achievement in skills and understanding, it is suggested that the instructor take charge of the booklets at the beginning of the term and distribute the tests as needed. The tests take on special importance because of the self-correcting character of exercises in the programmed method of instruction.

Two parallel tests—Form A and Form B—are provided for each of the twelve units. A comprehensive Pre-Test, a Final Test, and two parallel Halfway Tests are also included.

Whether a test is given to individual students or to the entire class at the same time depends on how the textbook is used. If students proceed at their own rates until they complete the entire book, individual testing will be necessary. If the class waits until all students complete a given unit before proceeding to the next, the class may be tested simultaneously.

The inclusion of parallel tests—Form A and Form B—gives the test booklet great flexibility in meeting the needs of a specific class and in providing for various classroom situations. You may use the two forms in a variety of ways.

1. Unit Test A may be used as a pre-test to discover whether or not a unit needs to be studied by the class as a whole or only by certain students. When the score indicates a need for the unit, Test B may be used to test achievement after the unit has been completed.
2. After the completion of any unit, Test A may serve as a practice or warm-up test to indicate the student's readiness for the "official" test and, when necessary, to motivate further preparation for it.
3. Test A or Test B may be used as a "second-try" test with students who did not achieve satisfactory scores on their first test.
4. Tests A and B may be used with alternating rows to ensure independent work when such an arrangement seems desirable.
5. Tests A and B may be used with different classes.

Because the Pre-Test and Final Test are parallel in coverage and weighting, they may be regarded as two versions of the same test.

For each section of the various tests, scoring values are indicated on the basis of 100 percent for the complete test. In general, each item is marked on an "all right" or "all wrong" basis, with no credit for a partially correct answer, In sections that call for two-part answers, you may choose to allow half credit where one of the two answers is correct. It will be found much simpler, of course, to compute scores by discounting the errors from 100 percent rather than by adding credits for correct answers.

An Answer Key containing the answers to the tests is available upon request.

NAME_____ DATE_____ CLASS_____

PRE-TEST

After each statement write *True* or *False* in the space at the right.   [1 point each]

1 An adjective can modify a pronoun.   1 _____
2 An adjective can modify another adjective.   2 _____
3 Adverbs modify more kinds of words than adjectives.   3 _____
4 The object of a preposition can be a noun or a pronoun.   4 _____
5 A sentence can contain both an adjective phrase and an adverb phrase.   5 _____
6 A simple sentence may have a compound subject.   6 _____
7 Any clause makes good sense when it stands alone.   7 _____
8 An adverb clause can frequently be moved in a sentence.   8 _____
9 A clause signal is used to begin an adverb, not an adjective, clause.   9 _____
10 A sentence that can be divided into two or more separate sentences is a complex sentence.   10 _____

Indicate the pattern of each sentence by writing one of the following letters: [2 points each]

A = Subject — Verb
B = Subject — Verb → Direct Object
C = Subject — Linking Verb ← Subject Complement

11 The rules of the game have been changed.   11 _____
12 The speaker looked nervous.   12 _____
13 We ordered flowers for the party.   13 _____
14 Mount McKinley is the highest peak in North America.   14 _____
15 A car in the right lane skidded.   15 _____

Eliminate the *and* by changing the italicized statement to the kind of word group indicated in the parentheses. Rewrite each sentence.   [3 points each]

16 *We went to bed late,* and we couldn't get up for breakfast.   (adverb clause) _____
_____

17 The batter hit a fly ball, and *I caught it.*   (adjective clause) _____
_____

18 *He realized that he was lost,* and he asked us for directions.   (*-ing* word group) _____
_____

Tests for English 2600   1

19 Mother spoke softly, and *she was very angry.*   (adverb clause) _____

20 In Venice we saw the Grand Canal, and *it is the city's main thoroughfare.*   (appositive) _____

Identify each word group, using the following letters: [1 point each]

F = Fragment   S = Sentence   R S = Run-on Sentence

21 We watched the chess match, it ended in a draw.   **21** _____
22 Being of sound mind and sound body.   **22** _____
23 First she studied medicine, then she turned to law.   **23** _____
24 We drove to San Diego Bay, which is an inlet of the Pacific.   **24** _____
25 A day that I shall never forget.   **25** _____
26 After I saw the movie, I decided to read the book.   **26** _____

Copy the correct word in each pair.   [1 point each]

27 We (*run, ran*) out of gas on the way to the beach.   **27** _____
28 Ann had (*lain, laid*) her books on the end table.   **28** _____
29 We should have (*taken, took*) the last exit.   **29** _____
30 Dad has (*driven, drove*) cross-country twice.   **30** _____
31 Why don't you (*leave, let*) her do her work?   **31** _____
32 Our puppy has (*tore, torn*) the bedroom curtains.   **32** _____
33 After lunch Uncle Lou (*laid, lay*) down for a nap.   **33** _____
34 The axle of the car was (*broken, broke*) in the accident.   **34** _____
35 Harry's aunt (*give, gave*) him a watch for his birthday.   **35** _____
36 I should have (*written, wrote*) sooner.   **36** _____
37 Here (*is, are*) the books I promised you.   **37** _____
38 Jean always has (*a, an*) excuse for being late.   **38** _____
39 The bus company must (*of, have*) changed the schedule.   **39** _____
40 One of our neighbors (*owns, own*) a dachshund.   **40** _____
41 The cello or the viola (*need, needs*) to be tuned.   **41** _____
42 The windows of my apartment (*face, faces*) south.   **42** _____
43 Oil (*doesn't, don't*) mix with water.   **43** _____
44 Each of the dresses (*were, was*) unusual.   **44** _____
45 These shoes fit (*well, good*).   **45** _____
46 This peach is (*riper, more riper*) than the other.   **46** _____
47 Marge plays the piano (*skillful, skillfully*).   **47** _____
48 The situation looks (*bad, badly*) to me.   **48** _____
49 We were served (*prompt, promptly*) in the restaurant.   **49** _____
50 (*Their, They're*) luggage was sent to the wrong hotel.   **50** _____
51 They made (*theirselves, themselves*) at home.   **51** _____
52 Do you know (*whose, who's*) bicycle this is?   **52** _____
53 The Mortons and (*we, us*) rented a cabin for the summer.   **53** _____

PRE-TEST (Continued)

54 Let's keep this a secret between you and (*I, me*).   54 _____
55 The Bartons and (*they, them*) took the same train.   55 _____
56 (*We, Us*) girls collected clothing for the flood victims.   56 _____
57 John is as fine a musician as (*him, he*).   57 _____
58 I (*couldn't, could*) hardly catch my breath.   58 _____
59 We didn't see (*anybody, nobody*) we knew at the party.   59 _____

Write the letter of the sentence in which capitals are used <u>correctly</u>.   [2 points each]

60 a. Every summer my aunt Margaret attends the Shakespeare Festival in Central park.
     b. Every summer my Aunt Margaret attends the Shakespeare Festival in Central Park.
     c. Every Summer my Aunt Margaret attends the Shakespeare festival in Central Park.   60 _____

61 a. During the Christmas Concert, our Chorus presented selections from *A Ceremony Of Carols*.
     b. During the christmas concert, our chorus presented selections from *A Ceremony of carols*.
     c. During the Christmas concert, our chorus presented selections from *A Ceremony of Carols*.   61 _____

62 a. The Beacon Construction Company finished the left wing of Kingsley Junior High School on Thursday.
     b. The Beacon Construction company finished the left wing of Kingsley Junior High school on Thursday.
     c. The Beacon construction company finished the left wing of Kingsley junior high school on thursday.   62 _____

Write the letter of the sentence that does <u>not</u> have an error in the use of apostrophes.   [2 points each]

63 a. Our dog does'nt like to eat its food alone.
     b. Our dog doesn't like to eat its food alone.
     c. Our dog doesn't like to eat it's food alone.   63 _____

64 a. The children's clothes cost more than our's.
     b. The childrens' clothes cost more than ours.
     c. The children's clothes cost more than ours.   64 _____

65 a. All the students' compositions are on the teacher's desk.
     b. All the student's compositions are on the teachers' desk.
     c. All the students' compositions are on the teachers' desk.   65 _____

Write the letter of the sentence which is correctly punctuated. [2 points each]

66 a. On March 10, 1876, Alexander Graham Bell inventor of the telephone transmitted the first spoken message electrically.
   b. On March 10, 1876, Alexander Graham Bell, inventor of the telephone, transmitted the first spoken message electrically.
   c. On March 10, 1876, Alexander Graham Bell inventor of the telephone, transmitted the first spoken message electrically. 66 _____

67 a. While the roast was in the oven, Mrs. Gray drew up the outline, wrote the preface, and completed an opening chapter for her new book.
   b. While the roast was in the oven, Mrs. Gray drew up the outline, wrote the preface, and completed an opening chapter, for her new book.
   c. While the roast was in the oven Mrs. Gray drew up the outline, wrote the preface, and completed an opening chapter, for her new book. 67 _____

68 a. Harry is right of course, to defend his position, but he should give us some more facts to go on.
   b. Harry is right, of course, to defend his position but he should give us some more facts to go on.
   c. Harry is right, of course, to defend his position, but he should give us some more facts to go on. 68 _____

69 a. Dr. Fredericks opened her wallet and took out her driver's license, and voter's registration card.
   b. Dr. Fredericks opened her wallet, and took out her driver's license and voter's registration card.
   c. Dr. Fredericks opened her wallet and took out her driver's license and voter's registration card. 69 _____

70 a. Please remember Susan, that you must lower the heat after the soup comes to a boil.
   b. Please remember, Susan, that you must lower the heat after the soup comes to a boil.
   c. Please remember, Susan, that you must lower the heat, after the soup comes to a boil. 70 _____

71 a. Marie said "I'd like a second helping of pie."
   b. Marie said, "I'd like a second helping of pie".
   c. Marie said, "I'd like a second helping of pie." 71 _____

72 a. "How can you eat so much?" asked Jerry.
   b. "How can you eat so much? asked Jerry."
   c. "How can you eat so much," asked Jerry? 72 _____

NAME_____ DATE_____ CLASS_____

UNIT 1-A THE VERB AND ITS SUBJECT

After each statement write *True* or *False* in the space at the right.   [2 points each]

1 A sentence might consist of only two words.   1 _____
2 The subject of a sentence usually comes after, not before, the predicate.   2 _____
3 The most important word in the predicate is the verb.   3 _____
4 Changing a sentence from present to past, or from past to present, helps one to
   find the subject.   4 _____
5 A noun but not a pronoun can be used as the subject of a sentence.   5 _____
6 A pronoun can be used to avoid repeating a noun.   6 _____

Indicate in the space at the right whether each word group is the subject of a sentence, the predicate of a sentence, or a complete sentence.   Use the following letters: [2 points each]

   S = Subject   P = Predicate   S P = Subject and Predicate (Complete Sentence)

7   the rooms on the top floor   7 _____
8   we agreed   8 _____
9   criticized the policies of the government   9 _____
10 the rich soil of this fertile valley   10 _____
11 the tunnel under the Hudson River   11 _____
12 the fair lasted for an entire week   12 _____
13 printed a complete report of the game   13 _____
14 practiced for their next game   14 _____
15 the shape of Italy resembles a boot   15 _____
16 the loss of life on our highways   16 _____

Indicate the simple subject and the verb in each sentence by writing, under the proper heading, the letter of each word you select.   [2 points for each sentence]

                                                        Subject   Verb
17 A small fire quickly spreads to a large area.   17 _____   _____
    A   B   C   D   E   F G H I
18 Everybody in the room talked at once.   18 _____   _____
    A   B C   D   E   F   G
19 The voice with a smile wins.   19 _____   _____
    A   B   C   D   E   F
20 The local train stops at every small town.   20 _____   _____
    A   B   C   D   E   F   G   H
21 Tornadoes often occur there in the spring.   21 _____   _____
    A   B   C   D   E F   G

Tests for English 2600

		Subject	Verb

22 A harpist never uses his little fingers.
    A   B   C   D   E   F   G   22 _____ _____

23 Three or four students usually did most of the work.
    A   B   C   D   E   F   G H   I J   23 _____ _____

24 A woman in the next seat overheard my remark.
    A   B   C D   E   F   G   H   I   24 _____ _____

25 Lightning follows the path of least resistance.
    A   B   C   D   E   F   G   25 _____ _____

26 The last few customers finally left the store.
    A   B   C   D   E   F   G   H   26 _____ _____

27 The shortage of skilled mechanics became serious.
    A   B   C   D   E   F   G   27 _____ _____

28 The previous owner of the car certainly knew its defects.
    A   B   C   D   E   F   G   H   I   J   28 _____ _____

In one of each pair of sentences, the italicized word is used as a noun and in the other as a verb. Identify each word, using the following letters: [2 points for each word]

          N = Noun   **V = Verb**

29 a. The last *show* ends very late.   29 a. _____
     b. Her grades *show* her ability.   b. _____

30 a. Dick's *run* won the game.   30 a. _____
     b. The students *run* the meetings.   b. _____

31 a. The boys *fish* from the bridge.   31 a. _____
     b. The big *fish* shook the hook.   b. _____

32 a. These companies *pay* high wages.   32 a. _____
     b. The high *pay* attracts many workers.   b. _____

33 a. *Oil* reduces friction.   33 a. _____
     b. They *oil* all moving parts.   b. _____

34 a. The students *print* their own paper.   34 a. _____
     b. The small *print* strains one's eyes.   b. _____

Identify each italicized word, using the following letters: [2 points for each sentence]

          N = Noun   **P = Pronoun**

35 *Many* lost their *jobs*.   35 _____ _____
36 There were *tracks* in the *snow*.   36 _____ _____
37 The first *locker* is *mine*.   37 _____ _____
38 The *store* will exchange *them*.   38 _____ _____
39 *Some* even stood on *chairs*.   39 _____ _____
40 A *man* left *these* at our door.   40 _____ _____
41 Each *person* ate *several*.   41 _____ _____
42 Why did *you* let *yourself* forget?   42 _____ _____
43 *Which* goes to the *stadium*?   43 _____ _____
44 There is *room* for only *one*.   44 _____ _____

NAME_____ DATE_____ CLASS_____

UNIT 1-B THE VERB AND ITS SUBJECT

After each statement write *True* or *False* in the space at the right.   [2 points each]

1 The most important word in the predicate is usually a noun or a pronoun.   1 _____
2 The predicate of a sentence must always contain a verb.   2 _____
3 It is better to find the subject before you find the verb.   3 _____
4 When you change a sentence from present to past, or from past to present, the verb is likely to change its form.   4 _____
5 If a word is a noun, it can be used as the subject of a sentence.   5 _____
6 A pronoun is generally more definite than a noun.   6 _____

Indicate in the space at the right whether each word group is the subject of a sentence, the predicate of a sentence, or a complete sentence. Use the following letters: [2 points each]

S = Subject   P = Predicate   S P = Subject and Predicate (Complete Sentence)

7 looked like a checkerboard from the plane   7 _____
8 the car ahead of us suddenly stopped   8 _____
9 the foundation of the building   9 _____
10 starts easily in all kinds of weather   10 _____
11 the number of parts in an airplane engine   11 _____
12 delivers our milk every day   12 _____
13 I apologized   13 _____
14 the price of admission to the exhibit   14 _____
15 struck out with three players on base   15 _____
16 one half of all American families own their own homes   16 _____

Indicate the simple subject and the verb in each sentence by writing, under the proper heading, the letter of each word you select.   [2 points for each sentence]

                                                                                Subject   Verb

17 Dave seldom came to our meetings.   17 _____ _____
    A   B   C D E   F
18 The magnificent colors of the sunset soon faded.   18 _____ _____
    A   B   C   D E   F   G H
19 The chocolate in my pocket melted.   19 _____ _____
    A   B   C D   E   F
20 A most amusing incident happened to me today.   20 _____ _____
    A   B   C   D   E   F G H
21 The new light at this corner prevents many accidents.   21 _____ _____
    A   B   C   D   E   F   G   H   I

Tests for English 2600

	Subject	Verb

22 A very severe storm recently struck our county.
    A B C D E F G H
22 _____ _____

23 Mistletoe grows on many different kinds of trees.
    A B C D E F G H
23 _____ _____

24 The store promptly and cheerfully refunded my money.
    A B C D E F G H
24 _____ _____

25 Some large industries find useful jobs for the blind.
    A B C D E F G H I
25 _____ _____

26 Many old and tattered magazines lay around the doctor's office.
    A B C D E F G H I J
26 _____ _____

27 The picture on the cover sold many magazines.
    A B C D E F G H
27 _____ _____

28 People from all over the world attended the convention.
    A B C D E F G H I
28 _____ _____

In one of each pair of sentences, the italicized word is used as a noun and in the other as a verb. Identify each word, using the following letters: [2 points for each word]

N = Noun   V = Verb

29 a. The *paint* spilled on the floor.   29 a. _____
    b. We *paint* our boat every summer.   b. _____

30 a. The lamp *lights* the room.   30 a. _____
    b. The bright *lights* dazzled our eyes.   b. _____

31 a. His humorous *talk* amused the audience.   31 a. _____
    b. The students *talk* about sports.   b. _____

32 a. The *cook* called us for dinner.   32 a. _____
    b. Some men *cook* as a hobby.   b. _____

33 a. Several *dishes* broke in the crash.   33 a. _____
    b. Mother *dishes* the ice cream.   b. _____

34 a. The leaves *cover* the grass.   34 a. _____
    b. The *cover* fell off the book.   b. _____

Identify each italicized word, using the following letters: [2 points for each sentence]

N = Noun   P = Pronoun

35 The *driver* blamed *himself*.   35 _____ _____
36 *We* like our new *neighbors*.   36 _____ _____
37 A *letter* came for *her* today.   37 _____ _____
38 The *company* enlarged its *factory*.   38 _____ _____
39 *Some* took shelter under an *awning*.   39 _____ _____
40 *Which* is the more expensive *car*?   40 _____ _____
41 *Peter* offered his *opinion* of the book.   41 _____ _____
42 *It* knows more tricks than *ours*.   42 _____ _____
43 Borrow a *pen* if you don't have *one*.   43 _____ _____
44 *This* would make a better *gift*.   44 _____ _____

NAME_____ DATE_____ CLASS_____

UNIT 2-A PATTERNS OF THE SIMPLE SENTENCE

After each statement write *True* or *False* in the space at the right.   [2 points each]

1. Some action verbs make complete statements about their subjects.   1 _____
2. A direct object usually means the same person or thing as the subject of the sentence.   2 _____
3. An indirect object, if present, stands between the verb and the direct object.   3 _____
4. If a verb is used as a linking verb, we can generally put some form of the verb *be* in its place.   4 _____
5. After every linking verb we expect to find either a direct object or a subject complement.   5 _____
6. A subject complement is so called because it describes or identifies the subject of the sentence.   6 _____

Write the letter of the sentence in which the italicized word is used as an indirect object.   [2 points each]

7. a. We taught several new tricks to our *dog*.
   b. We taught our *dog* several new tricks.   7 _____
8. a. The company offered *Dad* a much better job.
   b. The company offered to my *Dad* a much better job.   8 _____
9. a. The club bought their *church* a new organ.
   b. The club bought a new organ for their *church*.   9 _____
10. a. My uncle taught Spanish to *himself* at home.
    b. My uncle taught *himself* Spanish at home.   10 _____
11. a. I ordered my *friend* some printed stationery.
    b. I ordered for my *friend* some printed stationery.   11 _____

Identify each italicized word, using the following letters: [3 points for each sentence]

D O = Direct Object   I O = Indirect Object   S C = Subject Complement

12. Tom was the old *butler* in the last act.   12 _____
13. The noise of the motors frightens the *fish*.   13 _____
14. My friend did *me* a great *favor*.   14 _____ _____
15. The congestion on the highways has become very *serious*.   15 _____
16. The women were discussing *books* and *sports*.   16 _____ _____
17. Good science fiction is both *interesting* and *instructive*.   17 _____ _____
18. I carried the *letter* in my pocket for several days.   18 _____
19. Cartoons show *people* their *weaknesses* very forcefully.   19 _____ _____

Indicate the pattern of each sentence by writing one of the following letters: [3 points each]

- A = Subject — Action Verb
- B = Subject — Action Verb → Direct Object
- C = Subject — Action Verb — Indirect Object → Direct Object
- D = Subject — Linking Verb ← Subject Complement

20 Some great discoveries of science were accidental. 20 ____
21 Mrs. Jenkins showed us her beautiful guitar. 21 ____
22 The captain of the other team objected. 22 ____
23 The decision of the referee surprised the fans. 23 ____
24 My mother made the boys some delicious doughnuts. 24 ____
25 The dreams of today become the realities of tomorrow. 25 ____
26 Several of the circus animals escaped. 26 ____
27 The governor appointed several female judges. 27 ____

Copy the two words in each line that are forms of the helping verb *be*. [1 point for each word]

28	do	was	are	not	must	28 ____ ____
29	am	can	will	were	seem	29 ____ ____
30	may	is	had	did	been	30 ____ ____

Copy the two words in each line that may be used as helping verbs. [1 point for each word]

31	never	will	only	should	then	31 ____ ____
32	have	soon	make	become	could	32 ____ ____
33	did	still	can	really	always	33 ____ ____
34	lose	may	surely	almost	shall	34 ____ ____
35	and	stay	might	would	seem	35 ____ ____
36	must	very	then	has	more	36 ____ ____

Indicate the simple subject (or subjects) and the verb (or verbs) in each sentence by writing, under the proper headings, the letters of the words you select. [2 points for each sentence]

Subject(s) Verb(s)

37 A tired old lion was lying in the corner of the cage. 37 ____ ____
   A B   C   D   E   F   G H I J K L

38 Water evaporates from the earth and forms clouds. 38 ____ ____
   A   B   C   D E F   G   H

39 A freshman or a sophomore had seldom won this prize. 39 ____ ____
   A   B   CD   E   F   G   H   I J

40 The early show must have started already. 40 ____ ____
   A   B   C   D   E   F   G

41 We suddenly saw the signal and stopped at once. 41 ____ ____
   A   B   C   D   E   F   G H I

42 The smoke and water had damaged the merchandise. 42 ____ ____
   A   B   C   D   E   F   G   H

NAME_____ DATE_____ CLASS_____

UNIT 2-B PATTERNS OF THE SIMPLE SENTENCE

After each statement write *True* or *False* in the space at the right.   [2 points each]

1. Every action verb must be completed by a direct object.   1 _____
2. A word that receives the action of the verb or shows the result of the action is a direct object.   2 _____
3. When an indirect object is present, it stands between the verb and the direct object.   3 _____
4. An indirect object is always used with the word *to* or *for*.   4 _____
5. A linking verb can generally make a complete statement about its subject.   5 _____
6. A subject complement is so called because it completes the meaning of the predicate and describes or identifies the subject.   6 _____

Write the letter of the sentence in which the italicized word is used as an indirect object.   [2 points each]

7. a. I sold *John* my old camera.
    b. I sold my old camera to *John*.   7 _____
8. a. Helen showed to *us* her collection of photographs.
    b. Helen showed *us* her collection of photographs.   8 _____
9. a. Mr. Seely built a ping-pong table for his *children*.
    b. Mr. Seely built his *children* a ping-pong table.   9 _____
10. a. His success brought *him* no happiness.
    b. His success brought no happiness to *him*.   10 _____
11. a. Herb saved for his *friends* several seats in the fifth row.
    b. Herb saved his *friends* several seats in the fifth row.   11 _____

Identify each italicized word, using the following letters: [3 points for each sentence]

   D O = Direct Object   I O = Indirect Object   S C = Subject Complement

12. The company is building a new *factory*.   12 _____
13. The first three innings of the game were very *dull*.   13 _____
14. Sugar gives a *person* quick *energy*.   14 _____ _____
15. The weather station records the *speed* and *direction* of the wind.   15 _____ _____
16. Football is a very complicated *game*.   16 _____
17. George drew *me* a *map* of the route.   17 _____ _____
18. The street seemed unusually *quiet* and *peaceful*.   18 _____ _____
19. A whale can hold its *breath* for more than twenty minutes.   19 _____

Indicate the pattern of each sentence by writing one of the following letters: [3 points each]

  A = Subject — Action Verb
  B = Subject — Action Verb → Direct Object
  C = Subject — Action Verb — Indirect Object → Direct Object
  D = Subject — Linking Verb ← Subject Complement

20 The heavy downpour flooded many streets. 20 _____
21 The farmer showed us the best place to hunt. 21 _____
22 At this point, the audience laughed. 22 _____
23 The beginnings of language are very mysterious. 23 _____
24 Greg wrote his teacher a letter of apology. 24 _____
25 The population of our state has increased. 25 _____
26 Even large animals fear army ants. 26 _____
27 Ignorance is the mother of prejudice. 27 _____

Copy the two words in each line that are forms of the helping verb *be*. [1 point for each word]

28 can   am   got   was   has   28 _____ _____
29 are   seem   must   been   came   29 _____ _____
30 will   not   is   did   were   30 _____ _____

Copy the two words in each line that may be used as helping verbs. [1 point for each word]

31 soon   has   kept   then   can   31 _____ _____
32 never   became shall   should always 32 _____ _____
33 must   almost could   out   from   33 _____ _____
34 very   will   often   only   would   34 _____ _____
35 may   still   again   might   surely 35 _____ _____
36 when   did   were   first   more   36 _____ _____

Indicate the simple subject (or subjects) and the verb (or verbs) in each sentence by writing, under the proper headings, the letters of the words you select. [2 points for each sentence]

                                                    Subject(s)   Verb(s)
37 Terry must have forgotten my address.   37 _____ _____
     A   B   C   D   E F
38 The catcher and the pitcher had argued about the play. 38 _____ _____
     A   B   C   D   E   F   G   H   I   J
39 James laughed and cried at the same time.   39 _____ _____
     A   B   C   D   E F   G   H
40 Soap and water will not remove all spots.   40 _____ _____
     A   B   C   D   E   F   G   H
41 Few movies about circus life have been failures. 41 _____ _____
     A   B   C   D   E   F   G   H
42 Then the chemist slipped and nearly dropped the tray. 42 _____ _____
     A   B   C   D   E   F   G   H   I

NAME_____ DATE_____ CLASS_____

UNIT 3-A THE WORK OF MODIFIERS

After each statement write *True* or *False* in the space at the right. [2 points each]

1 An adjective can modify a verb. 1 _____
2 An adjective can be used as a subject complement after a linking verb. 2 _____
3 An adverb can modify a verb, an adjective, or another adverb. 3 _____
4 An adjective is more movable than an adverb. 4 _____
5 *Very, so, quite,* and *too* are adjectives, not adverbs. 5 _____
6 A word that tells *when, where, how,* or *how much* about a verb is an adverb. 6 _____
7 Every preposition requires an object. 7 _____
8 The object of a preposition is usually an adjective. 8 _____
9 A prepositional phrase contains a subject and a verb. 9 _____
10 Prepositional phrases can serve as modifiers in the same way that adjectives and adverbs do. 10 _____

Identify each italicized word by writing *Adjective* or *Adverb* in the spaces at the right.
[2 points for each sentence]

11 *Mature* people *seldom* lose their tempers. 11 _____ _____
12 I am *extremely sorry* about losing your book. 12 _____ _____
13 The *new* pupil walked *confidently* to the board. 13 _____ _____
14 My *first* year of high school was the *hardest*. 14 _____ _____
15 The witness answered my questions *quite truthfully*. 15 _____ _____

Indicate the class of the word that would fit into each space by writing *Adjective* or *Adverb* in the space at the right. Do not supply the modifiers. [2 points each]

16 We took a . . . walk before dinner. 16 _____
17 Ms. Ross treats all her customers . . . . 17 _____
18 This winter has been . . . cold. 18 _____
19 His car was going in the . . . direction. 19 _____
20 He . . . refused to move his car. 20 _____
21 My punctuation of the sentence was . . . . 21 _____
22 One should read directions . . . carefully. 22 _____
23 The coat looks too . . . for you. 23 _____
24 I can't study well in a . . . room. 24 _____
25 Lois should write her family . . . frequently. 25 _____

Copy the prepositional phrase in each sentence. [2 points each]

26 The figures on the check had been altered.
27 The trailer was swaying behind the car.
28 A strange dog ran through our flower beds.
29 The string around the package was broken.
30 In bad weather, the team practices indoors.
31 The family above us was very noisy.
32 Our paper was delivered by the boy's father.
33 The ball rolled under a passing car.
34 The value of money is constantly changing.
35 Several members jumped to their feet and protested.

26 _____
27 _____
28 _____
29 _____
30 _____
31 _____
32 _____
33 _____
34 _____
35 _____

Write the word that each italicized prepositional phrase modifies. [2 points each]

36 The space *between the two houses* was very narrow.
37 I found this picture *in an old book*.
38 The boy *beside me* was munching popcorn.
39 *During the evening* a light snow fell.
40 I sent the letter *to the wrong address*.
41 The day *after Christmas* seemed very dull.
42 Mr. Dietz greeted me *with a hearty handshake*.
43 The reason *for his absence* seemed very ridiculous.

36 _____
37 _____
38 _____
39 _____
40 _____
41 _____
42 _____
43 _____

Indicate how each italicized prepositional phrase is used by writing *Adjective* or *Adverb* in the space at the right. [2 points each]

44 Parts *for this old model* are hard to find.
45 Some people put salt *on fruit*.
46 *For several seconds* the fans held their breath.
47 Smoke *from many factories* contaminates the air.
48 Luisa enjoys any story *about sports*.
49 *At three o'clock* the dismissal bell rings.
50 He answered the questions *with no hesitation*.

44 _____
45 _____
46 _____
47 _____
48 _____
49 _____
50 _____

NAME_____ DATE_____ CLASS_____

UNIT 3-B THE WORK OF MODIFIERS

After each statement write *True* or *False* in the space at the right. [2 points each]

1 An adverb can modify another adverb.
2 An adjective can modify another adjective.
3 An adverb can modify an adjective, but an adjective cannot modify an adverb.
4 An adjective can be used as a subject complement after a linking verb.
5 An adjective can modify more classes of words than an adverb.
6 An adjective is generally more movable than an adverb.
7 A word that tells *when, where,* or *how* about a verb is an adjective.
8 A prepositional phrase always begins with a preposition.
9 Prepositional phrases can serve as modifiers in the same way that adjectives and adverbs do.
10 The object of a preposition is usually a verb.

1 _____
2 _____
3 _____
4 _____
5 _____
6 _____
7 _____
8 _____
9 _____
10 _____

Identify each italicized word by writing *Adjective* or *Adverb* in the spaces at the right.
[2 points for each sentence]

11 I *recently* saw an *unusual* movie.
12 The *young* trees are growing *rapidly*.
13 *This* book looks *interesting*.
14 Dad *always* eats his meals *fast*.
15 Bob was *rather indefinite* about his plans.

11 _____ _____
12 _____ _____
13 _____ _____
14 _____ _____
15 _____ _____

Indicate the class of the word that would fit into each space by writing *Adjective* or *Adverb* in the space at the right. Do not supply the modifiers. [2 points each]

16 The house was too . . . for our family.
17 Jerry . . . refused to recite the poem.
18 I received my . . . grade in English.
19 The dog seemed . . . hungry.
20 I should have counted my change . . . carefully.
21 The child's . . . remark amused the family.
22 Our kitchen is bright and . . . .
23 The lake was . . . rough on Sunday.
24 A car was approaching on the . . . side of the road.
25 . . . the line of cars began to move.

16 _____
17 _____
18 _____
19 _____
20 _____
21 _____
22 _____
23 _____
24 _____
25 _____

Tests for English 2600

Some of the following sentences contain one prepositional phrase; some contain two phrases. Copy each phrase on a separate line. [2 points for each sentence]

26 The women spent the day hunting for antiques.   26 _____

27 We grew tomatoes in a space behind our garage.   27 _____

28 There was a picket fence between the two yards.   28 _____

29 We learn much history from the letters of soldiers.   29 _____

30 The band played a stirring military march by Sousa.   30 _____

31 Ms. Chavez looked at my paper and shook her head.   31 _____

32 We stood under an awning during the storm.   32 _____

33 All the students except Matt had finished the test.   33 _____

34 After the meeting, the parents walked around the halls.   34 _____

35 I was discussing the new movie with my friend.   35 _____

Write the word that each italicized prepositional phrase modifies. [2 points each]

36 I showed the outline *to my teacher*.   36 _____
37 This popular song has the flavor *of an old ballad*.   37 _____
38 The drive *through the mountains* is very picturesque.   38 _____
39 I completed my theme *before class*.   39 _____
40 The painter placed the ladder *against the roof*.   40 _____
41 The address *on the envelope* was not legible.   41 _____
42 We towed the other car *with a heavy rope*.   42 _____
43 The bridge *across the stream* was swept away.   43 _____

Indicate how each italicized prepositional phrase is used by writing Adjective or Adverb in the space at the right. [2 points each]

44 The ball went right *through the window*.   44 _____
45 Officials are investigating the cause *of the crash*.   45 _____
46 *At ten o'clock* the late show will begin.   46 _____
47 The chapter *about banking* was difficult to read.   47 _____
48 Elmer recited his lines *with little expression*.   48 _____
49 *For several hours* they discussed politics.   49 _____
50 The letter *from his uncle* contained a check.   50 _____

NAME_____ DATE_____ CLASS_____

UNIT 4-A BUILDING BETTER SENTENCES

If the sentence is compound, In the space provided, write the word that should be followed by a comma, and also write the needed comma. If it is not compound, write the letters N C (Not Compound). [2 points each]

1 Lena played in the first half but dropped out of the game because of a slight injury to her back.

2 Lena played in the first half but a slight injury to her back forced her out of the game.

3 He came to this country in 1946 and his family arrived the following year.

4 He came to this country in 1946 and brought over his family the following year.

5 Shall I reply to this letter or simply ignore it?

6 Shall I reply to this letter or is it better simply to ignore it?

1 _____
2 _____
3 _____
4 _____
5 _____
6 _____

One of each of the following pairs of compound sentences is good because it combines similiar ideas of equal importance. The other is poor because it combines unlike ideas. Write the letter of the <u>good</u> sentence.   [2 points each]

7 a. I invited Doris to the game, and she is my friend's sister.
   b. I invited Doris to the game, but she had another date.

8 a. The game was exciting, and Dad picked us up in his car.
   b. The game was exciting, and the crowd was enthusiastic.

9 a. We didn't want the picture, but Mother couldn't refuse it.
   b. We didn't want the picture, but Mrs. Foltz thought it was very unusual.

10 a. Fewer workers are needed on farms, and farmers work long hours.
   b. Fewer workers are needed on farms, and many people take factory jobs.

11 a. The car was three years old, but it looked just like new.
   b. The car was three years old, and it had a new set of tires.

7 _____
8 _____
9 _____
10 _____
11 _____

Write the conjunction which expresses the meaning more clearly.   [2 points each]

12 The tree is small, *(and, but)* it will grow rapidly.
13 It was after midnight, *(and, but)* gas stations were closed.
14 I put a dime in the slot, *(and, but)* no candy came out.
15 Ms. Kane had made up her mind, *(and, but)* nothing would change it.
16 Mr. Kling is seventy years old, *(and, but)* he looks much younger.

12 _____
13 _____
14 _____
15 _____
16 _____

Tests for English 2600   17

Identify each italicized clause by writing *Adjective* or *Adverb* in the space at the right. [2 points each]

17 One should not interrupt a person *who is counting something*. 17 _____
18 *As soon as I begin to speak*, my nervousness disappears. 18 _____
19 We sold our piano *because none of us could play it*. 19 _____
20 The company *whose bid is lowest* will get the contract. 20 _____
21 The Newbergs moved *so that they would be closer to a school*. 21 _____
22 The directions *that came with the kit* were confusing. 22 _____

Eliminate the *and* by changing the italicized statement to the kind of word group indicated in the parentheses. Rewrite each sentence. [6 points each]

23 *Pete got to the corner*, and he turned in the wrong direction. (adverb clause) _____

24 Some people have fancy signatures, and *they are hard to read*. (adjective clause) _____

25 *Dave has driven for years*, and he has never had an accident. (adverb clause) _____

26 Larry was brought up by an aunt, and *she was very kind to him*. (adjective clause) _____

27 I wandered about the grounds, and *I admired the beds of flowers*. (-ing word group) _____

28 Joe sent the bill to Mr. Sims, and *he was the owner of the car*. (appositive) _____

Write the letter of the sentence that answers each question. [5 points each]

29 Which sentence shows the relationship between the two ideas most clearly?
   a. The bus broke down, and we were late for school.
   b. Because the bus broke down, we were late for school.
   c. Although the bus broke down, we were late for school. 29 _____
30 In which sentence is *whistling* used as an adjective?
   a. The whistling of the wind sounded weird.
   b. The wind was whistling weirdly.
   c. The whistling wind sounded weird. 30 _____
31 Which sentence contains an *-ing* word group?
   a. Luke, standing at the window, saw the lightning strike.
   b. Luke, who was standing at the window, saw the lightning strike.
   c. While Luke was standing at the window, he saw the lightning strike. 31 _____
32 Which sentence contains an appositive?
   a. Toby, who is the team's mascot, amused the fans.
   b. Toby, the team's mascot, amused the fans.
   c. Toby is the team's mascot, and he amused the fans. 32 _____

NAME_____ DATE_____ CLASS_____

UNIT 4-B BUILDING BETTER SENTENCES

If the sentence is compound, in the space provided, write the word that should be followed by a comma, and also write the needed comma. If it is not compound, write the letters N C (Not Compound). [2 points each]

1. Mr. Worthington bought a box of candy for his wife but he ate most of it himself.
2. Mr. Worthington bought a box of candy for his wife but ate most of it himself.
3. The bus ride was long and monotonous and tired the children.
4. The bus ride was long and monotonous and the children became very restless.
5. We must buy a new car or repair our old one.
6. The advertising must be truthful or our newspaper will not print it.

1 _____
2 _____
3 _____
4 _____
5 _____
6 _____

One of each of the following pairs of compound sentences is good because it combines similar ideas of equal importance. The other is poor because it combines unlike ideas. Write the letter of the <u>good</u> sentence. [2 points each]

7. a. The suit was a bargain, but I had spent all my money.
   b. The suit was a bargain, and my friend had one like it.
8. a. Ken needed money for college, and his uncle owned a gas station.
   b. Ken needed money for college, and his uncle gave him a job.
9. a. We had turkey for dinner, and I prefer the dark meat.
   b. Dad prefers the light meat, and I prefer the dark.
10. a. Sally swims with great speed, and her stroke is flawless.
    b. Sally swims with great speed, and she has a new swimsuit.
11. a. Both teams are good, and the competition is keen.
    b. Both teams are good, and we beat Baxter High last year.

7 _____
8 _____
9 _____
10 _____
11 _____

Write the conjunction which expresses the meaning more clearly. [2 points each]

12. Boyd is excellent in English, (*and, but*) math has always troubled him.
13. I wrote the store a letter, (*and, but*) they answered it promptly.
14. Gibson is a good mechanic, (*and, but*) his prices are reasonable.
15. The painting is valued at a million dollars, (*and, but*) it is not for sale.
16. Gloria and Frank went by plane, (*and, but*) Kurt and Sue preferred to go by car.

12 _____
13 _____
14 _____
15 _____
16 _____

Tests for English 2600

Identify each italicized clause by writing *Adjective* or *Adverb* in the space at the right. [2 points each]

17 *When a union and a company cannot agree*, a strike may occur.　　17 _____
18 We have a number of customers *who telephone their orders*.　　18 _____
19 I prayed for snow *so that I could try out my new skis*.　　19 _____
20 Vic has a new watch *which tells the day of the month*.　　20 _____
21 The woman *whose recipe won first prize* was not in the audience.　　21 _____
22 I always read her articles *although I frequently disagree with her*.　　22 _____

Eliminate the *and* by changing the italicized statement to the kind of word group indicated in the parentheses. Rewrite each sentence. [6 points each]

23 *We have had little rain*, and the crops will be poor. (adverb clause) _____

24 I got the advice of a friend, and *he knows a lot about cars*. (adjective clause) _____

25 John never gains weight, and *he is a big eater*. (adverb clause) _____

26 We gave the bike to a child, and *his father is out of work*. (adjective clause) _____

27 *I heard of his success*, and I sent him a telegram. (*-ing* word group) _____

28 The record was broken by Bill Knapp, and *he is a graduate of our school*. (appositive) _____

Write the letter of the sentence that answers each question. [5 points each]

29 Which sentence shows the relationship between the two ideas most clearly?
 a. Because I read the story twice, I missed the point.
 b. Although I read the story twice, I missed the point.
 c. I read the story twice, and I missed the point.　　29 _____
30 In which sentence is *clanging* used as an adjective?
 a. The church bells were clanging noisily.
 b. The clanging of the church bells awakened us.
 c. We were awakened by the clanging church bells.　　30 _____
31 Which sentence contains an *-ing* word group?
 a. The children stood in line, waiting for the theater to open.
 b. The children who were waiting for the theater to open stood in line.
 c. While they were waiting for the theater to open, the children stood in line.　　31 _____
32 Which sentence contains an appositive?
 a. Ms. Fritch, who is a retired lawyer, judged our speech contest.
 b. Ms. Fritch judged our speech contest, and she is a retired lawyer.
 c. Ms. Fritch, a retired lawyer, judged our speech contest.　　32 _____

UNIT 5-A UNDERSTANDING THE SENTENCE UNIT

Identify each of the two word groups by writing the following letters in the spaces at the right:
[2 points for each numbered item]

F = Fragment   S = Sentence

1. I should much prefer to send Gloria something unusual. Like a box of fine gems.
2. After a day of strenuous or tiresome work. Most people enjoy some form of recreation.
3. Expecting to meet his friend. Harold drove to the airport.
4. Without slowing down. Or signaling other drivers.
5. We once owned a most unusual cat. Whose name was Chick.
6. If there is any difference between these two colors. I can't see it.
7. Cheese is very nutritious. And costs less than meat.
8. Don't look for lost opportunities. Someone else has found them.
9. Whenever we mention our dog's name. He pricks up his ears.
10. Bolivia is named after Simón Bolívar. One of the great heroes of South America.

Correct each run-on sentence by writing a period and the capitalized word which should follow it. If the sentence is correct, write the word *Correct*.   [2 points each]

11. My camera was not expensive, it cost only a few dollars.
12. If you oil the fan, it will run more quietly.
13. Most of the children seldom buy anything, they just like to wander around.
14. If the squirrel should fail to dig up the buried nut, an oak tree will start to grow.
15. It was the fault of his parents, who should have refused such an unreasonable request.
16. If we clean the car, then we can sell it more easily.
17. We cleaned the car, then we advertised it in the paper.
18. Mother felt very sorry for the old peddler, she bought some trifle from him.
19. On the first day at sea, we walked around the great ship, exploring all the decks.
20. It was my first game of the season, therefore, I was slightly nervous and overanxious.

Tests for English 2600

Identify each word group, using the following letters: [2 points each]

F = Fragment   S = Sentence   R S = Run-on Sentence

21 The young people danced, the older people visited.   21 _____
22 The Hutzels have five children, three boys and two girls.   22 _____
23 Which made me think that he was only joking.   23 _____
24 We took the new road, it saved us several miles.   24 _____
25 If you take the new road, it will save you several miles.   25 _____
26 A small radio that fits conveniently into your pocket.   26 _____
27 In comparison with older drivers who have had more experience.   27 _____
28 I had my hair cut, then I discovered that I had no money.   28 _____
29 Although I have heard this story many times, it still amuses me.   29 _____
30 Grabbing his suitcase and running for the train.   30 _____
31 This is not the original statue, it is only a copy.   31 _____
32 An attractive plant that flowers all summer.   32 _____
33 Our neighbors were having a noisy party, therefore we couldn't sleep.   33 _____
34 My report was about Sir Alexander Fleming, the discoverer of penicillin.   34 _____

Write the letter of the <u>one correct</u> line that does not contain a fragment or run-on sentence error: [4 points each]

35 a. I laughed. Until the tears rolled down my face.
    b. I laughed until the tears rolled down my face.
    c. Laughing until the tears rolled down my face.   35 _____
36 a. The artist first makes a rough sketch. And then fills in the details.
    b. The artist first makes a rough sketch. Then she fills in the details.
    c. The artist first makes a rough sketch, then she fills in the details.   36 _____
37 a. We got permission from Mr. Boyer, who owns the property.
    b. We got permission from Mr. Boyer. The owner of the property.
    c. Mr. Boyer owns the property, he gave us permission to use it.   37 _____
38 a. Jim attended summer school. Because he needed additional credits.
    b. Jim attended summer school. To earn additional credits that he needed.
    c. Jim attended summer school to earn additional credits that he needed.   38 _____
39 a. Helen had a bad cold. Therefore, she didn't go swimming.
    b. Having a bad cold. Helen didn't go swimming.
    c. Helen had a bad cold, therefore she didn't go swimming.   39 _____
40 a. Being an expert lawyer. Sue was offered several jobs.
    b. Sue is an expert lawyer, she was offered several jobs.
    c. Because Sue is an expert lawyer, she was offered several jobs.   40 _____
41 a. We traded in our car, it needed too many repairs.
    b. We traded in our car. Since it needed too many repairs.
    c. We traded in our car. It needed too many repairs.   41 _____
42 a. The Eskimo women prepare the skins by chewing them until they are soft.
    b. The Eskimo women prepare the skins. By chewing them until they are soft.
    c. The Eskimo women prepare the skins by chewing them. Until they are soft. 42 _____

NAME_____ DATE_____ CLASS_____

UNIT 5-B UNDERSTANDING THE SENTENCE UNIT

Identify each of the two word groups by writing the following letters in the spaces at the right:
[2 points for each numbered item]

        F = Fragment   S = Sentence

1. Because Arlene stands too far from the plate. She takes too many called strikes.
2. Steve held the attention of the audience. From his very first sentence.
3. After a jet plane breaks through the sound barrier. The pilot hears no noise.
4. The driver tried to pass a truck. And misjudged the distance.
5. Leaving Ken in charge of the class. Ms. Ames left the room.
6. Without mentioning any names. Or embarrassing anybody.
7. As we rounded the curve. The car went dangerously close to the edge of the mountain.
8. My mother was writing a letter. My father was reading the paper.
9. I was born in Montreal. The largest city in Canada.
10. Mother was cooking asparagus. Which my brother doesn't like.

Correct each run-on sentence by writing a period and the capitalized word which should follow it. If the sentence is correct, write the word *Correct*.   [2 points each]

11. The small engine is economical, it uses very little gas.
12. At the time my parents moved to Huntsville, it was only a small town.
13. Roy doesn't listen, he just waits for a chance to talk about his own experiences.
14. While we were waiting for a bus, a friend came along in his car.
15. Ernie had an injured shoulder, which prevented him from pitching.
16. I received several issues of the magazine, then it stopped coming.
17. If you have tried your best, then no one can blame you for not succeeding.
18. The audience kept on applauding, they wanted an encore.
19. A lobster lurks in its underground cave, waiting to seize a passing fish.
20. The water pressure was low, therefore the fire got out of control.

Tests for English 2600

Identify each word group, using the following letters: [2 points each]

F = Fragment   S = Sentence   R S = Run-on Sentence

21 Without catching a single fish or even getting a bite. 21 _____
22 A large box was delivered on Monday, the day before my birthday. 22 _____
23 Which seems a poor reason for dropping out of school. 23 _____
24 Some like hot cereal, others prefer cold cereal. 24 _____
25 If a lawn mower is dull, it will do a poor job. 25 _____
26 The lawn mower was dull, it did a poor job. 26 _____
27 If you forbid children to go to this movie, they will want to go all the more. 27 _____
28 A tired old horse that could hardly stand up. 28 _____
29 He was planning to bake a cake, then he decided to buy one. 29 _____
30 Driving around the block and looking for a place to park. 30 _____
31 Although we had a comfortable lead at the beginning of the ninth inning, we lost the game. 31 _____
32 A book that tells all about skiing and other sports. 32 _____
33 I read the question hastily, therefore I got the wrong answer. 33 _____
34 We spent a week at Aspen, one of the best ski resorts in the West. 34 _____

If you did not use semicolons, how many sentences would you make of the three word groups printed after each number? Write 1, 2, or 3 in the space at the right.   [4 points each]

35 I tried the front door   then I tried the back door   it was locked, too. 35 _____
36 After I tried the front door   I tried the back door   which was also locked. 36 _____
37 Since our examinations come next week   social life is at a standstill   students are burying their noses in books. 37 _____
38 Colette stayed home   she was writing a theme   which had to be finished by morning. 38 _____
39 You see the lightning   before you hear the thunder   although both occur at the same time. 39 _____
40 It rained on Election Day   therefore many voters failed to vote   such people do not deserve good government. 40 _____
41 We heard a scraping sound   it turned out to be a branch   rubbing against the roof. 41 _____
42 Since my father is an importer   I plan to study two foreign languages   French and Spanish. 42 _____

UNIT 6-A USING VERBS CORRECTLY

Write in the space at the right the proper past form of each verb in parentheses. Watch for any form of the helping verbs *have* and *be*, which must be followed by the helper form of the main verb. [2 points each]

1 The boys soon (*run*) out of money.
2 This car has (*give*) us a lot of trouble.
3 My brother had already (*go*) to bed.
4 This historical novel was (*write*) for children.
5 I have never (*see*) so many cats.
6 Someone had (*eat*) all the cookies.
7 This picture was (*take*) when I was six.
8 The driver (*do*) his best to prevent the accident.
9 Miss James had often (*speak*) of her niece.
10 This car must have been (*drive*) without any oil.
11 Later we (*see*) smoke pouring from the windows.
12 The boat had (*break*) away from the dock.
13 These berries were (*fly*) here from California.
14 The customer soon (*come*) back for his change.
15 I have (*know*) many boys like Jerry.
16 Wanda has (*grow*) two inches during the past year.
17 His companion was (*throw*) through the windshield.
18 One of the robins had (*fall*) from its nest.
19 You would have (*do*) the same thing.
20 The clerk (*give*) me a free sample.
21 This job must have (*take*) a lot of patience.
22 The player had (*run*) to the wrong goal.
23 Our principal has just (*fly*) to Washington.
24 Mr. Brooks (*give*) me a good grade in English.
25 Carmen has (*write*) a skit for the program.
26 Higgens (*throw*) the ball to third base.
27 The other man had (*drive*) through a red light.
28 The pencil was (*break*) when you gave it to me.
29 Have you (*see*) the new model yet?
30 This tearoom was (*run*) by two English sisters.
31 It was too late when the doctor finally (*come*).
32 I (*lie*) back in the barber chair and relaxed.
33 The dog had (*lie*) on the porch all morning.
34 Vic (*lay*) all his cards on the table.
35 Archie forgot where he had (*lay*) the car keys.

Tests for English 2600

36 Phil (*sit*) and waited for his turn. 36 _____
37 Anita had (*set*) a wet glass on my new book. 37 _____
38 We (*sit*) on the grass and ate our sandwiches. 38 _____
39 The cost of living (*rise*) again last year. 39 _____
40 The water level had (*rise*) during the night. 40 _____

Copy the correct word in the space at the right. [2 points each]

41 You can (*lie, lay*) your things on this chair. 41 _____
42 Why don't you (*lie, lay*) in the sun? 42 _____
43 I could (*have, of*) eaten the entire pie. 43 _____
44 First (*leave, let*) the milk come to a boil. 44 _____
45 The taxi (*let, left*) me off at the wrong hotel. 45 _____
46 This should (*of, have*) been reported to the police. 46 _____
47 Why don't you (*leave, let*) someone else have a turn? 47 _____
48 Dad must (*have, of*) forgotten to mail the letter. 48 _____
49 The clerk said, "If your mother doesn't like the dress, you may (*bring, take*) it back." 49 _____
50 Ms. Cruz gave me a report to (*bring, take*) to the office. 50 _____

UNIT 6-B USING VERBS CORRECTLY

Write in the space at the right the proper past form of each verb in parentheses. Watch for any form of the helping verbs *have* and *be*, which must be followed by the helper form of the main verb.   [2 points each]

1 You should have (*see*) the expression on his face.
2 These grapes were (*grow*) in Ohio.
3 The mail (*come*) late this morning.
4 The dish was (*break*) when we unpacked it.
5 *The Diary of a Young Girl* was (*write*) by Anne Frank.
6 We should have (*take*) a picture of the party.
7 He must have (*drive*) at least ten miles out of his way.
8 Mr. Brock (*do*) most of the work himself.
9 Fresh vegetables are (*fly*) here from Florida.
10 The car soon (*run*) out of gas.
11 Tom should have (*eat*) his vegetables.
12 Some green apples had (*fall*) from the tree.
13 Juan must have (*do*) this job in a hurry.
14 Mr. Akashi (*give*) his entire library to the school.
15 I had (*speak*) to Miss Crane about my change in plans.
16 The pictures showed the damage that the storm had (*do*).
17 The package should have (*come*) this morning.
18 This television set has (*give*) us good service.
19 It was cold because our fire had (*go*) out.
20 I (*see*) the notice in yesterday's paper.
21 Several passengers were (*throw*) to the floor.
22 Inez should have (*run*) to second base.
23 Someone must have (*break*) this lock.
24 I wish I had (*know*) that the car was for sale.
25 Donna has (*write*) several short stories.
26 The stain (*come*) out in the wash.
27 Most of the berries were (*eat*) by the birds.
28 Ms. Bennett has (*fly*) her own plane for many years.
29 Peggy (*do*) her homework after dinner.
30 Mr. Hicks has (*come*) to collect for the insurance.
31 The child must have (*run*) all the way to school.
32 I (*lie*) back in my chair and relaxed.
33 Dad had (*lie*) down on the sofa for a nap.
34 Dick (*lay*) his books on a vacant seat.
35 Alva forgot where she had (*lay*) her keys.

Tests for English 2600

36 I (*sit*) and waited for the dentist to call me in. 36 _____
37 Ralph had (*sit*) on some wet paint. 37 _____
38 Sue had (*set*) the cake on a kitchen chair. 38 _____
39 Lena Trombley (*rise*) and walked to the window. 39 _____
40 The number of traffic deaths has (*rise*). 40 _____

Copy the correct word in the space at the right.   [2 points each]

41 I could (*have, of*) finished in another half hour. 41 _____
42 (*Lie, Lay*) down and go to sleep. 42 _____
43 Don't (*lie, lay*) your skates on the stairs. 43 _____
44 Why did you (*leave, let*) the potatoes burn? 44 _____
45 The police will not (*let, leave*) you park there. 45 _____
46 The family could (*of, have*) used the money more wisely. 46 _____
47 If you will (*bring, take*) me your radio, I'll fix it for you. 47 _____
48 Dad reminded me to (*take, bring*) the eggs back to the store. 48 _____
49 Andy (*left, let*) me off to pick up our groceries. 49 _____
50 I should (*have, of*) studied harder for the test. 50 _____

HBJ material copyrighted under notice appearing earlier in this work.

HALFWAY TEST-A (Units 1 through 6)

After each statement write *True* or *False* in the space at the right.   [1 point each]

1 Either an adverb or an adjective can modify a verb.   1 _____
2 Adverbs and adverb word groups are more movable than adjectives and adjective word groups.   2 _____
3 Every sentence must contain either a direct object, an indirect object, or a subject complement.   3 _____
4 The subject complement which follows a linking verb may be a noun or an adjective.   4 _____
5 A preposition always requires an object.   5 _____
6 A prepositional phrase always contains a verb.   6 _____
7 A compound sentence can be divided into two separate sentences.   7 _____
8 An adverb clause or an adjective clause makes complete sense by itself.   8 _____
9 A clause that modifies a noun or pronoun is an adverb clause.   9 _____
10 The clause signals *who* (*whom*, *whose*), *which*, and *that* are used to introduce adjective, not adverb, clauses.   10 _____

Indicate the simple subject (or subjects) and the verb (or verbs) in each sentence by writing under the proper headings the letters of the words you select.   [1 point for each sentence]

                                                                                       Subject(s)   Verb(s)

11 Someone should have reported the accident.   11 _____ _____
    A   B   C   D   E   F

12 The earliest train for Atlanta leaves at 9:00 A.M.   12 _____ _____
    A   B   C   D   E   F   G   H I

13 Lee and the new boy from Philadelphia soon became
    A   B   C   D   E   F   G   H   I
   very good friends.   13 _____ _____
   J   K   L

14 Their methods of agriculture are very primitive.   14 _____ _____
    A   B   C   D   E   F   G

15 The fishermen wear hip boots and fish in the streams.   15 _____ _____
    A   B   C   D   E   F   G H I   J

16 The new owner of the theater has been losing money.   16 _____ _____
    A   B   C   D   E   F   G   H   I   J

17 In those days, most people seldom traveled very far.   17 _____ _____
    A   B   C   D   E   F   G   H I

18 His mother and his father have gone to Florida for
    A   B   C   D   E   F   G   H   I   J
   their vacation.   18 _____ _____
    K   L

19 Andy reached for a light switch and tripped over a chair.   19 _____ _____
    A   B   C D   E   F   G   H   I J K

Tests for English 2600

Indicate the pattern of each sentence by writing one of the following letters in the space at the right:
[1 point each]

   A = Subject — Verb
   B = Subject — Verb → Direct Object
   C = Subject — Linking Verb ← Subject Complement

20 All the members of the committee agreed.   20 _____
21 The driver might have been asleep.   21 _____
22 The woman in front of me wore a big hat.   22 _____
23 Some of our guests arrived early.   23 _____
24 I have never seen a more enthusiastic audience.   24 _____
25 The weather seemed too cold for a picnic.   25 _____
26 You can judge a person's character by his or her driving.   26 _____
27 Many of the vacationists had already left.   27 _____
28 These plants are not suitable for this climate.   28 _____

Read the following sentence. Then identify the class of words to which each italicized word belongs by writing in the space at the right the letter of the class of words in Column B which corresponds with the word in Column A.   [1 point each]

We can *often see* ships *and* a *lighthouse in* the *distance on very clear days.*

	A		B
29	We	a.	noun
30	can	b.	pronoun
31	often	c.	verb
32	see	d.	adjective
33	and	e.	adverb
34	lighthouse	f.	preposition
35	in	g.	conjunction
36	distance		
37	on		
38	very		
39	clear		
40	days		

29 _____
30 _____
31 _____
32 _____
33 _____
34 _____
35 _____
36 _____
37 _____
38 _____
39 _____
40 _____

Each sentence contains both an adjective and an adverb in italics. Write the adverb in the space at the right.   [1 point each]

41 This *small* town is growing *rapidly*.   41 _____
42 *Often* her remarks are quite *funny*.   42 _____
43 I lost weight *fast* on this *skimpy* diet.   43 _____
44 The *last* show ends *late*.   44 _____
45 The *impatient* customer walked *out*.   45 _____
46 The mink is a *very ferocious* animal.   46 _____

NAME_____ DATE_____ CLASS_____

HALFWAY TEST-A (Continued)

Copy each prepositional phrase and write the word that it modifies. [1 point for each sentence]

	Phrase	Modifies
47 The title of the book aroused my interest.	47 _____	_____
48 I changed my hat in a hurry.	48 _____	_____
49 The trip through the mine took almost an hour.	49 _____	_____
50 At noon the church bells rang.	50 _____	_____
51 The first prize was a ticket to the World Series.	51 _____	_____
52 The dog hid under the sofa.	52 _____	_____

Write the letter of the better compound sentence in each pair. [1 point each]

53 a. Boston is an interesting city, and my cousin lives there.
    b. Boston is an interesting city, and there is much to see.   53 _____

54 a. The recipe was simple, and I could follow it easily.
    b. The recipe was simple, and everyone enjoyed the cake.   54 _____

55 a. I nominated Rosa, and Paul seconded the nomination.
    b. I nominated Rosa, and the election is next week.   55 _____

56 a. The roads were good, and we passed through several towns.
    b. The roads were good, and the scenery was interesting.   56 _____

Combine each pair of sentences by changing the italicized sentence to the kind of word group indicated in the parentheses. [4 points each]

57 *Joe took the clock apart.* He couldn't put it together again. (adverb clause) _____
_____

58 I gave my seat to a lady. *She kept dropping her packages.* (adjective clause) _____
_____

59 He wrote to the mayor. *He complained about the bus service.* (-*ing* word group) _____
_____

60 Louise invited me to visit her. *She is my cousin from Texas.* (appositive) _____
_____

Tests for English 2600

Identify each word group, using the following letters: [1 point each]

F = Fragment   S = Sentence   R S = Run-on Sentence

61 The weather is perfect, it is neither too hot nor too cold.   61 _____
62 Roy did his best trick, pouring water from an empty bottle.   62 _____
63 A person who was never too busy to help others.   63 _____
64 One of the greatest athletes of this century.   64 _____
65 First the public demands large cars, then it wants small cars. 65 _____
66 Gary was always borrowing a pencil and paper.   66 _____
67 Because I needed spending money for the summer.   67 _____
68 The dress was slightly soiled, therefore the price was reduced. 68 _____
69 If a car swerves when stopping, the brakes need adjusting.   69 _____
70 Thinking only of his own comfort and convenience.   70 _____

Write in the spaces at the right the correct past form of each of the two verbs in parentheses. [1 point for each verb]

71 We (*sit*) in the library and (*do*) our homework.   71 _____ _____
72 Someone had (*take*) my picture after I had (*fall*) asleep.   72 _____ _____
73 I (*see*) the watch that the church had (*give*) to our minister.   73 _____ _____
74 Irene (*run*) to the mailbox with the letter she had just (*write*).   74 _____ _____
75 We (*let, left*) them pay for the window they had (*break*).   75 _____ _____
76 I would have (*speak*) to Manuel if I had (*know*) he was there.   76 _____ _____
77 Dad had (*eat*) his dinner and had just (*lie*) down to rest.   77 _____ _____
78 Mr. Grant should have (*rise*) when the judge (*come*) into the room.   78 _____ _____
79 I have (*drive*) to California, and I have also (*fly*) there.   79 _____ _____

HALFWAY TEST-B (Units 1 through 6)

After each statement write *True* or *False* in the space at the right. [1 point each]

1 Every action verb must be completed by a direct object. 1 _____
2 When there is an indirect object in a sentence, it always follows the direct object. 2 _____
3 An adverb can modify an adjective, but an adjective cannot modify an adverb. 3 _____
4 An adjective can modify more classes of words than an adverb. 4 _____
5 Prepositional phrases can be used like adjectives and adverbs to modify various words in a sentence. 5 _____
6 Adverbs and adverb word groups are more movable than adjectives and adjective word groups. 6 _____
7 We do not generally expect to find the conjunction *and, but,* or *or* in a compound sentence. 7 _____
8 A clause, like a sentence, always contains a subject and a verb. 8 _____
9 The clause signals *when, because, if,* and *although* generally introduce adjective clauses. 9 _____
10 A clause that modifies a verb is an adverb clause. 10 _____

Indicate the simple subject (or subjects) and the verb (or verbs) in each sentence by writing under the proper headings the letters of the words you select. [1 point for each sentence]

                                                                                Subject(s)   **Verb(s)**

11 Anyone could have made this same mistake. 11 _____ _____
    A   B   C   D   E   F   G
12 The effects of the Industrial Revolution were tremendous. 12 _____ _____
    A   B   C   D   E   F   G   H
13 Pete's voice and appearance seem perfect for this part. 13 _____ _____
    A   B   C   D   E   F   G   H   I
14 All complaints about the service should be reported to the
    A   B   C   D   E   F   G   H   I   J
   manager. 14 _____ _____
   K
15 We looked at the menu and left the restaurant. 15 _____ _____
    A   B   C   D   E   F   G   H   I
16 Small events can sometimes change the history of the world. 16 _____ _____
    A   B   C   D   E   F   G   H   J
17 In our school, the principal often visits various classes. 17 _____ _____
    A B   C   D   E   F   G   H   I
18 Most trees and shrubs have already shed their leaves. 18 _____ _____
    A   B   C   D   E   F   G   H   I
19 Many shoppers go from store to store and compare prices. 19 _____ _____
    A   B   C   D   E   F   G   H   I   J

Indicate the pattern of each sentence by writing one of the following letters in the space at the right:
[1 point each]

$$A = \text{Subject — Verb}$$
$$B = \text{Subject — Verb} \rightarrow \text{Direct Object}$$
$$C = \text{Subject — Linking Verb} \leftarrow \text{Subject Complement}$$

20 The ending of this movie surprised most people. 20 _____
21 Suddenly one of the chairs collapsed. 21 _____
22 Your film may have been too old. 22 _____
23 The leader of the guerrilla band surrendered. 23 _____
24 Seat belts have saved the lives of many motorists. 24 _____
25 The furniture seemed too large for the room. 25 _____
26 A movie about circus life has seldom failed. 26 _____
27 The solar battery converts sunlight directly into electricity. 27 _____
28 Automobiles are the main source of air contamination. 28 _____

Read the following sentence. Then identify the class of words to which each italicized word belongs by writing in the space at the right the letter of the class of words in Column B which corresponds with the word in Column A. [1 point each]

I *recently* read a *most* *fascinating* *book* *about* *ants* *and* bees *which* I *would* *recommend* *to* *you*.

A		B	
29	recently	a. noun	29 _____
30	most	b. pronoun	30 _____
31	fascinating	c. verb	31 _____
32	book	d. adjective	32 _____
33	about	e. adverb	33 _____
34	ants	f. preposition	34 _____
35	and	g. conjunction	35 _____
36	which		36 _____
37	would		37 _____
38	recommend		38 _____
39	to		39 _____
40	you		40 _____

Each sentence contains both an adjective and an adverb in italics. Write the adverb in the space at the right. [1 point each]

41 *Soon* the store was quite *crowded*. 41 _____
42 An *important* battle was fought *there*. 42 _____
43 The *elderly* man was walking *briskly*. 43 _____
44 I can play *better* with a *heavier* racket. 44 _____
45 Monday was an *extremely* hot day. 45 _____
46 Our *first* guests arrived *early*. 46 _____

HALFWAY TEST-B (Continued)

Copy each prepositional phrase and write the word that it modifies. [1 point for each sentence]

	Phrase	Modifies
47 The girl from Sweden spoke perfect English.	47 _____	_____
48 For a moment we expected an explosion.	48 _____	_____
49 Have you ever read a story by Thurber?	49 _____	_____
50 The catcher threw the ball to first base.	50 _____	_____
51 The shape of this flower is unusual.	51 _____	_____
52 We watched the takeoff with great interest.	52 _____	_____

Write the letter of the better compound sentence in each pair. [1 point each]

53 a. The party was called off, and everyone was disappointed.
    b. The party was called off, and I was planning to wear a gypsy costume.   53 _____

54 a. The telephone rang, and I was in the basement.
    b. The telephone rang, and I rushed to answer it.   54 _____

55 a. I didn't recognize Don, and he was with his parents.
    b. I didn't recognize Don, and he didn't recognize me.   55 _____

56 a. The program was good, and everyone enjoyed it.
    b. The program was good, and I drove home with my friends.   56 _____

Combine each pair of sentences by changing the italicized sentence to the kind of word group indicated in the parentheses. [4 points each]

57 *Jiggs barks ferociously.* He has never bitten anyone. (adverb clause) _____

58 The directions are very simple. *They come with each kit.* (adjective clause) _____

59 We walked up and down the aisle. *We looked for vacant seats.* (-ing word group) _____

60 Mr. Voss identified the note. *He is a handwriting expert.* (appositive) _____

Identify each word group, using the following letters: [1 point each]

F = Fragment   S = Sentence   R S = Run-on Sentence

61 Including a radio, a heater, and other accessories.   61 _____
62 Hash is not made, it just accumulates.   62 _____
63 Although every turn in the road is clearly marked.   63 _____
64 Rita owns sixty acres of land, which she inherited from her grandfather.   64 _____
65 We swam for a while, then we lay on the beach.   65 _____
66 Especially during the winter months when the snow is heavy.   66 _____
67 If you offer too many excuses, people will begin to doubt you.   67 _____
68 A job which takes at least an entire day.   68 _____
69 I had read the book, therefore I was eager to see the movie.   69 _____
70 We strolled through the Farmers' Market, a place of great activity on Saturday morning.   70 _____

Write in the spaces at the right the correct past form of each of the two verbs in parentheses. [1 point for each verb]

71 The man (*come*) to pick up the stove we had (*give*) him.   71 _____ _____
72 Mother had (*grow*) tired of the picture and had (*throw*) it away.   72 _____ _____
73 We (*see*) the Pelham Road bus coming and (*run*) to catch it.   73 _____ _____
74 I could have (*write*) a better report if I had (*take*) more time.   74 _____ _____
75 We (*sit*) at the dining-room table and (*do*) our algebra problems.   75 _____ _____
76 A large branch had (*break*) off and had (*fall*) on a parked car.   76 _____ _____
77 If you had (*speak*) to me, I would have (*let, left*) you use my ticket.   77 _____ _____
78 He had (*eat*) a heavy dinner and had (*lie*) down for a nap.   78 _____ _____
79 I would have (*rise*) early if I had (*know*) that you planned to go fishing.   79 _____ _____

NAME_____ DATE_____ CLASS_____

UNIT 7-A AGREEMENT OF SUBJECT AND VERB

Copy the verb that agrees with its subject. [2 points each]

1. There (*was, were*) no corrections on my paper.
2. The game (*don't, doesn't*) start until eight o'clock.
3. My interest in animals (*goes, go*) back to my childhood.
4. The results of this experiment (*were, was*) amazing.
5. July or August (*are, is*) the best time for a vacation.
6. Every one of these buttons (*brings, bring*) in a different station.
7. A scratch or a small cut sometimes (*cause, causes*) serious infection.
8. The rules for this game (*doesn't, don't*) make much sense to me.
9. One of the faucets (*needs, need*) fixing.
10. Here (*is, are*) the names of my customers.
11. Each one of these children (*has, have*) an interesting hobby.
12. There (*weren't, wasn't*) any tickets left for us.
13. The marks on the pavement (*shows, show*) where you skidded.
14. The weight of the crackers (*were, was*) printed on the package.
15. Either of these coats (*fits, fit*) you very well.
16. The size and the price of our yearbook (*has, have*) been increased.
17. This lamp (*don't, doesn't*) give enough light.
18. The pearls in this necklace (*are, is*) genuine.
19. Where (*is, are*) the saucers for these cups?
20. Every one of these plants (*needs, need*) water.

1 _____
2 _____
3 _____
4 _____
5 _____
6 _____
7 _____
8 _____
9 _____
10 _____
11 _____
12 _____
13 _____
14 _____
15 _____
16 _____
17 _____
18 _____
19 _____
20 _____

The italicized verb in each of the following sentences agrees with its subject. Now suppose that you were to insert the words in parentheses at the point indicated by the caret (∧). If a change in the verb would be necessary, write the correct form on the blank line. If the verb would remain the same, write the word *Correct*. [2 points each]

21. ∧ These pictures *are* remarkable. (The clearness of)
22. Peggy ∧ *stays* with the children. (or her sister)
23. The profit ∧ *goes* to the school. (from these games)
24. Fresh air ∧ *stimulates* the appetite. (and exercise)
25. The doctor ∧ *plans* to see you tonight. (or her assistant)
26. ∧ The children *help* with the housework. (Every one of)
27. Where *is* ∧ the paper? (the envelopes and)
28. Either one ∧ *unlocks* the door. (of these keys)

21 _____
22 _____
23 _____
24 _____
25 _____
26 _____
27 _____
28 _____

Tests for English 2600   37

29 A minister ∧ *offers* the opening prayer.   (, a priest, or a rabbi)   29 _____
30 Much time ∧ *was* spent on the decorations.   (and effort)   30 _____
31 Each ∧ *takes* a half-hour to do.   (of these problems)   31 _____
32 ∧ The boys *don't* live near school.   (Only one of)   32 _____
33 An automobile ∧ *goes* to the winner.   (, with a year's supply of gas,)   33 _____
34 ∧ These answers *are* correct.   (Either of)   34 _____
35 There *was* ∧ one girl on the committee.   (two boys and)   35 _____

Write the letter of the <u>one incorrect</u> sentence in each group.   [6 points each]

36 a. A knife and a spoon are all that you need.
   b. We soon found out that crime doesn't pay.
   c. Have either of the candidates answered our questions?   36 _____

37 a. Only one of the problems was difficult.
   b. A book or a magazine help to pass the time.
   c. The cost of the repairs was covered by insurance.   37 _____

38 a. Which one of these knobs controls the volume?
   b. Here are the directions for the game.
   c. The length of the theme really don't matter.   38 _____

39 a. The frequency of the commercials spoil the program.
   b. Each of my brothers plays a different instrument.
   c. What were his objections to our plan?   39 _____

40 a. The preparations for a party take much time.
   b. There was no numbers on the house.
   c. Every one of these posters deserves a prize.   40 _____

NAME_____ DATE_____ CLASS_____

UNIT 7-B AGREEMENT OF SUBJECT AND VERB

Copy the verb that agrees with its subject. [2 points each]

1. One of my friends (*knows, know*) the superintendent.
2. Mr. Phillips or Ms. Cole (*leads, lead*) the singing.
3. There (*is, are*) about thirty thousand stitches in a suit of clothes.
4. Parts for this foreign car (*was, were*) hard to get.
5. The title of this book (*doesn't, don't*) sound interesting.
6. Nearly every one of your sentences (*contain, contains*) an *and*.
7. His interest in horses (*go, goes*) back to his childhood.
8. A candy bar or a piece of fruit (*is, are*) not an adequate lunch.
9. There (*wasn't, weren't*) enough programs for everybody.
10. The customs of a people (*don't, doesn't*) change very rapidly.
11. The purpose of fuses (*is, are*) to prevent fires.
12. Each of these shirts (*have, has*) some slight defect.
13. Here (*are, is*) the tickets for the game.
14. The effects of this invention (*was, were*) tremendous.
15. Either of these cars (*are, is*) a good buy.
16. This cartoon (*doesn't, don't*) seem funny to me.
17. The first few chapters of the book (*build, builds*) up a lot of suspense.
18. Every one of the members (*were, was*) present.
19. The length and the width of the car (*has, have*) been increased.
20. Where (*are, is*) the attachments for the vacuum cleaner?

The italicized verb in each of the following sentences agrees with its subject. Now suppose that you were to insert the words in parentheses at the point indicated by the caret (∧). If a change in the verb would be necessary, write the correct form on the blank line. If the verb would remain the same, write the word *Correct*. [2 points each]

21. ∧ Our shrubs *need* trimming. (Every one of)
22. Do you know where my ∧ tools *are*? (box of)
23. The smoke ∧ *pollutes* the air. (from the factories)
24. A play ∧ *costs* too much. (or a concert)
25. The radio ∧ *costs* extra. (and the heater)
26. ∧ The windows *were* broken. (One of)
27. Corn ∧ *grows* well in this soil. (and wheat)
28. Either one ∧ *takes* you downtown. (of these buses)

Tests for English 2600

29 A king ∧ *counts* as ten. (, queen, or jack)   29 _____
30 Where *is* ∧ the thread? (the needles and)   30 _____
31 Each ∧ *has* a special job to do. (of the members)   31 _____
32 My father ∧ sometimes *helps* me with my math.   (or my mother)   32 _____
33 This pencil ∧ *sells* for one dollar. (, with a year's supply of lead,)   33 _____
34 *Are* ∧ you ready to give your report? (either of)   34 _____
35 ∧ This article *makes* you think. (The facts in)   35 _____

Write the letter of the <u>one incorrect</u> sentence in each group.   [6 points each]

36 a. This motor doesn't need to be oiled.
    b. Every one of these bolts need tightening.
    c. A teacher or a counselor sponsors each club.   36 _____
37 a. There was no concrete roads in those days.
    b. The rareness of these stamps makes them valuable.
    c. Has either of her brothers attended college?   37 _____
38 a. His idea of fun is bowling and roller skating.
    b. The cracks in the pavement let frost get in.
    c. A few drops of lemon juice adds to the flavor.   38 _____
39 a. A prize or a coupon come in each package.
    b. The selection of the right colors is most important.
    c. Her voice and her manner remind me of your sister.   39 _____
40 a. Here are your tickets for the game.
    b. Not one of our birthdays come during the summer.
    c. The saving in time and labor soon pays for the equipment.   40 _____

UNIT 8-A CHOOSING THE RIGHT MODIFIER

Copy the correct modifier in each sentence.   [2 points each]

1. Brush your teeth (*good, well*) after eating dinner.
2. Have you ever seen anyone drive more (*graceful, gracefully*)?
3. The new rules are (*stricter, more stricter*) than the old ones.
4. Ted's plan sounded (*foolish, foolishly*) to most of the members.
5. The price doesn't make (*no, any*) difference to him.
6. Would you like (*a, an*) omelet for breakfast?
7. I am thinking quite (*seriously, serious*) about going to college.
8. Which is (*farthest, farther*) south — Atlanta or Memphis?
9. The room looks (*different, differently*) with the new curtains.
10. Why did we spend our money so (*foolishly, foolish*)?
11. We didn't go (*nowhere, anywhere*) on the Fourth of July.
12. You should clean your room more (*thoroughly, thorough*).
13. Our new can opener works very (*good, well*).
14. Rayon is (*more cheaper, cheaper*) than real silk.
15. Uncle Ed calls on us quite (*regular, regularly*).
16. A field of sweet clover smells very (*pleasant, pleasantly*).
17. Borrow (*a, an*) onion from Mrs. Jacobson.
18. Mr. Diaz seemed much more (*cheerful, cheerfully*) than usual.
19. The boys wouldn't take (*nothing, anything*) for their help.
20. Clean your brush (*good, well*) before painting.
21. Mother felt (*terrible, terribly*) about the scratch on her new car.
22. I thought that his violin sounded (*terribly, terrible*).
23. Do you consider French or Spanish (*harder, hardest*)?
24. Mr. Casper held the baby very (*awkwardly, awkward*).
25. Our television set is working (*good, well*) again.
26. Dave is looking for (*an, a*) easier job.
27. Everything Linda does she does (*perfect, perfectly*).
28. This cake tastes very (*delicious, deliciously*) with cold milk.
29. Little Sandy (*could, couldn't*) hardly reach the shelf.
30. The new driver applied the brakes too (*sudden, suddenly*).
31. It was the (*driest, most driest*) speech I've ever heard.
32. Which is the (*ripest, riper*) of these two melons?
33. These scissors don't cut (*good, well*) anymore.
34. I should much prefer (*a, an*) earlier class.
35. This was the (*funniest, most funniest*) story I have ever read.

Tests for English 2600

Write the letter of the <u>one</u> sentence in each group in which the italicized word is <u>incorrect</u>. [6 points each]

36 a. You can't breathe *good* in high altitudes.
b. This record doesn't sound as *clear* as the other.
c. I felt very *happy* about my test score. **36** _____

37 a. Sonja plans to become *an* electrical engineer.
b. The doctor didn't find *anything* wrong with my eyes.
c. We *couldn't* hardly hear the last speaker. **37** _____

38 a. His car doesn't start *well* in cold weather.
b. Our boat was now leaking *bad*.
c. The color looks *different* at night. **38** _____

39 a. Do your new shoes feel *comfortable*?
b. Which is *larger* — the United States or Brazil?
c. The weather turns *more* cooler in September. **39** _____

40 a. This was the *difficultest* stunt I have ever seen.
b. Terry now knows her lines almost *perfectly*.
c. My friend wouldn't take *any* pay for his work. **40** _____

UNIT 8-B CHOOSING THE RIGHT MODIFIER

Copy the correct modifier in each sentence.   [2 points each]

1. David is (*more handier, handier*) in the kitchen than his sister.
2. We are living in this apartment only (*temporarily, temporary*).
3. He didn't do that dive very (*good, well*).
4. This little French restaurant didn't have (*any, no*) menu.
5. Motors run more (*economical, economically*) at moderate speeds.
6. Ms. Keeler gives quite (*generous, generously*) to charity.
7. The clerk proved himself (*an, a*) honest person.
8. Shake the bottle (*good, well*) before taking the medicine.
9. The collision damaged our car (*bad, badly*).
10. Do you consider French or Spanish (*harder, hardest*)?
11. My plan sounded (*sensible, sensibly*) to my parents.
12. A person can't drive too (*careful, carefully*) nowadays.
13. Dad never eats (*anything, nothing*) between meals.
14. The Panthers tried very (*desperately, desperate*) for a touchdown.
15. I can't hear (*good, well*) in the back of the auditorium.
16. The new road is (*safer, more safer*) than the old one.
17. Harold speaks so (*rapidly, rapid*) that he is hard to understand.
18. This perfume smells more (*expensively, expensive*) than the others.
19. Our best pitcher is now recovering from (*an, a*) operation.
20. Paul should have answered the phone more (*pleasant, pleasantly*).
21. I couldn't find my key (*nowhere, anywhere*).
22. Wash your hands (*well, good*) before handling your food.
23. Ernie felt (*sad, sadly*) about his dog's injury.
24. This story begins very (*interesting, interestingly*).
25. Your dress looks quite (*different, differently*) when worn with the jacket.
26. Which is (*largest, larger*) — Texas or Alaska?
27. My pen doesn't write (*well, good*) on this kind of paper.
28. I usually have (*an, a*) egg for breakfast.
29. The hot buttered popcorn tasted (*deliciously, delicious*).
30. The new driver stopped the bus too (*sudden, suddenly*).
31. The messenger (*could, couldn't*) hardly read the address.
32. Everything Martha does, she does very (*thoroughly, thorough*).
33. I prefer a (*more milder, milder*) cheese.
34. It was the (*delightfullest, most delightful*) trip I have ever taken.
35. The candidate took the news of her defeat quite (*calm, calmly*).

Write the letter of the <u>one</u> sentence in each group in which the italicized word is <u>incorrect</u>. [6 points each]

36 a. This family had moved into our neighborhood very *recently*.
     b. The car skidded *badly* when we took the curve.
     c. These apples *don't* scarcely have any flavor.   36 _____

37 a. I wouldn't leave *anything* valuable in my locker.
     b. Your voice sounds *differently* over the telephone.
     c. Which is *longer* — a yard or a meter?   37 _____

38 a. This engine runs *well* on ordinary gasoline.
     b. The salad tasted *peculiar* to me.
     c. It was the *terriblest* storm I have ever experienced.   38 _____

39 a. Hilda tried on both coats, but she didn't like *neither* one.
     b. Ramona felt *unhappy* about losing the contest.
     c. Have you ever seen *an* elephant dance?   39 _____

40 a. Walter looked *unhappy* about his report card.
     b. Nylon is *more* stronger than rayon.
     c. Barry has been dressing more *neatly* lately.   40 _____

NAME_____ DATE_____ CLASS_____

UNIT 9-A USING PRONOUNS CORRECTLY

If you were to put a pronoun in place of the dots, would you use a pronoun in the subject or the object form? Write the letter S for the subject form or the letter O for the object form in the space at the right.
[2 points each]

1 Mr. Harris found jobs for my brother and . . . . 1 _____
2 Bert and . . . found seats in the last row. 2 _____
3 I'm planning to go with Rita and . . . . 3 _____
4 The coach will use . . . boys in Friday's game. 4 _____
5 Nobody else worked as hard as . . . . 5 _____

Copy the correct pronoun in each sentence.   [2 points each]

6 Anna shot two more baskets than (*him, he*). 6 _____
7 I wish that this car were (*our's, ours*). 7 _____
8 We notified the Nortons and (*them, they*) of the meeting. 8 _____
9 The principal (*himself, hisself*) taught the class. 9 _____
10 Will they let (*we, us*) students use the pool? 10 _____
11 Sincerely (*your's, yours*). 11 _____
12 The Deckers or (*we, us*) can pick you up at the station. 12 _____
13 Coach Brock saved Stan and (*he, him*) for the last half. 13 _____
14 Between you and (*I, me*), Lynn paid too much for that flute. 14 _____
15 I now weigh almost as much as (*he, him*). 15 _____
16 (*Us, We*) Americans believe in equal opportunity. 16 _____
17 Both my sisters put (*themselves, theirselves*) through college. 17 _____
18 The girls and (*they, them*) changed seats. 18 _____
19 The accident cost us more than (*they, them*). 19 _____
20 I wonder where (*it's, its*) mother can be? 20 _____
21 The teacher gave extra help to (*us, we*) boys after class. 21 _____
22 I saw you walking with Leonard and (*her, she*). 22 _____
23 Uncle George took him and (*me, I*) to the game. 23 _____
24 Why don't you find (*yourself, your self*) a seat? 24 _____
25 The Milners don't eat as early as (*us, we*). 25 _____
26 We built the entire cottage (*ourselves, ourselfs*). 26 _____
27 See if there is any mail for Dad or (*I, me*). 27 _____
28 (*Us, We*) students should stand solidly behind our teams. 28 _____
29 (*She, Her*) and I were the last two girls in line. 29 _____
30 The gift from (*she, her*) and Juan came on Christmas Eve. 30 _____
31 The new rules apply to them as well as (*we, us*). 31 _____

32 Our cat was sunning (*it's self, itself*) on the roof of the garage. 32 _____
33 Why don't they try to sell (*theirs, their's*)? 33 _____
34 What did the coach say about (*us, we*) athletes? 34 _____
35 Norm and (*he, him*) share the same locker. 35 _____

Write the letter of the <u>one</u> sentence in each group in which the pronoun is <u>incorrect</u>.   [6 points each]

36 a. Floyd and I finally got the car started.
  b. I can't tie a bow tie as well as he.
  c. You should not judge a book by it's cover.   36 _____
37 a. Reggie considers himself an expert bowler.
  b. Us students should be loyal to our teams.
  c. Why don't you bring yours along, too?   37 _____
38 a. You and she should get along very well.
  b. The Borowskis built the entire garage theirselves.
  c. Hal's sudden friendliness looked suspicious to Roberta and me.   38 _____
39 a. Lucia enjoys cooking more than him.
  b. The success of the plan depends on us girls.
  c. I wouldn't trust Nancy or her with my secret.   39 _____
40 a. The game will settle the tie between Colby and us.
  b. They invited the Novaks and us to their cottage.
  c. We sent invitations to the Changs and they.   40 _____

UNIT 9-B USING PRONOUNS CORRECTLY

If you were to put a pronoun in place of the dots, would you use a pronoun in the subject or the object form? Write the letter S for the subject form or the letter O for the object form in the space at the right. [2 points each]

1. Why didn't you notify Clyde or . . . ?
2. Neither the Perrys nor . . . had heard the news.
3. . . . girls waited for over an hour.
4. I saved some seats for Karen and . . . .
5. The storm frightened Elton more than . . . .

Copy the correct pronoun in each sentence. [2 points each]

6. Ron doesn't live as far from school as (*we, us*).
7. You can ride to church with the Vernons or (*we, us*).
8. (*Your's, Yours*) truly.
9. The Guzmans and (*they, them*) are our closest neighbors.
10. Jimmy helped (*himself, hisself*) to another piece of cake.
11. My young brother usually tagged along behind (*we, us*) fellows.
12. Yukio and (*I, me*) happened to wear the very same shirts.
13. The flowers were sent by Lisa and (*her, she*).
14. (*Our's, Ours*) was only slightly damaged by the collision.
15. Was the crowd cheering them or (*us, we*)?
16. The explosion frightened the Crandalls more than (*we, us*).
17. I was sitting all by (*my self, myself*) in the last row.
18. The Morrises and (*us, we*) share the same party line.
19. My birthday is on the same day as (*her's, hers*).
20. We were surprised by (*its, it's*) reasonable price.
21. (*Him, He*) and I belong to the same club.
22. There was no room in the canoe for (*we, us*) boys.
23. The coach wanted Wallace and (*he, him*) to try out for track.
24. The children amused (*themselves, theirselves*) by asking riddles.
25. I have driven a car as long as (*him, he*).
26. We couldn't make out (*its, it's*) license number.
27. Why don't we also invite the Youngs and (*they, them*)?
28. Mother expected (*us, we*) girls to clean up after the party.
29. Dad refused to go to the cottage without Mother and (*me, I*).
30. Claudette and (*she, her*) were in charge of decorations.
31. The new fashions suit you much better than (*I, me*).

32 We found (*ourselves, ourselfs*) a good place to camp.   32 _____
33 Harley got eight more votes than (*him, he*).   33 _____
34 (*We, Us*) Americans believe in freedom of speech.   34 _____
35 Between you and (*me, I*), the accident was Barry's fault.   35 _____

Write the letter of the <u>one</u> sentence in each group in which the pronoun is <u>incorrect</u>.   [6 points each]

36 a. Ms. Kirk marked you and I absent today.
    b. We should consider changing its name.
    c. The boys found themselves on the wrong bus.   36 _____
37 a. You and he can meet us after school.
    b. We've won three games more than they.
    c. Our house is much smaller than their's.   37 _____
38 a. The principal asked Dale and him to serve on the committee.
    b. We don't keep our car as long as them.
    c. Sam's success was a great joy to Mr. Valenti and her.   38 _____
39 a. The Hartmans and we cleaned up the vacant lot.
    b. Why can't Jerry stay up as late as he?
    c. Several of we fellows offered to help her.   39 _____
40 a. Between you and me, the party was a failure.
    b. Raul papered the entire room hisself.
    c. Neither we nor anyone else remembered to bring a can opener.   40 _____

NAME_____   DATE_____   CLASS_____

UNIT 10-A HOW TO USE CAPITALS

Suppose that each of the following phrases occurred within a sentence. Write the letter of the <u>one</u> phrase in each group that is <u>correctly</u> printed.   [2 points each]

1   a. in World war II   b. in world war II   c. in World War II   1 _____
2   a. a Black magazine   b. a Black Magazine   c. a black magazine   2 _____
3   a. a lake in Sherman County   b. a lake in Sherman county
         c. a Lake in Sherman County   3 _____
4   a. a new Elementary school   b. a new elementary school
         c. a new Elementary School   4 _____
5   a. with freshie toothpaste   b. with Freshie Toothpaste
         c. with Freshie toothpaste   5 _____
6   a. from Major Larsen   b. from major Larsen   c. from major larsen   6 _____
7   a. every friday night   b. every Friday Night   c. every Friday night   7 _____
8   a. this German recipe   b. this German Recipe   c. this german recipe   8 _____
9   a. my Aunt Cathy and two cousins   b. my Aunt Cathy and two Cousins
         c. my aunt Cathy and two cousins   9 _____
10 a. a Ford dealer   b. a ford dealer   c. a Ford Dealer   10 _____
11 a. at Cody high school   b. at Cody High School   c. at Cody High school   11 _____
12 a. in the stevens memorial hospital   b. in the Stevens memorial hospital
         c. in the Stevens Memorial Hospital   12 _____
13 a. to a June Wedding   b. to a June wedding   c. to a june wedding   13 _____
14 a. by a hollywood studio   b. by a Hollywood Studio
         c. by a Hollywood studio   14 _____
15 a. the Northern pacific railroad   b. the Northern Pacific railroad
         c. the Northern Pacific Railroad   15 _____
16 a. the first day of Summer   b. the first day of summer
         c. the first Day of Summer   16 _____
17 a. at a New York hotel   b. at a New York Hotel
         c. at a New york hotel   17 _____
18 a. many Japanese christians   b. many Japanese Christians
         c. many japanese Christians   18 _____
19 a. to the American cancer society   b. to the American Cancer society
         c. to the American Cancer Society   19 _____
20 a. sang "The Old Folks at Home"   b. sang "The old folks at home"
         c. sang "The Old Folks At Home"   20 _____

Tests for English 2600

Copy with a small letter the one word in each line that should not be capitalized. [2 points each]

21	Canada	Baseball	Hanukkah
22	Spanish	Latin	Algebra
23	Measles	Coca-Cola	Indian
24	Baptist	Kansas	Engineer
25	English	Carnations	Buick
26	Poodle	February	Harvard
27	Wheaties	Wednesday	Flu
28	Biology	Bible	Eskimo
29	Irish	Saxophone	Asia
30	Chicago	Cadillac	Hamburgers

21 _____
22 _____
23 _____
24 _____
25 _____
26 _____
27 _____
28 _____
29 _____
30 _____

Write the letter of each word that should be capitalized. [4 points for each sentence]

31 His mother is recovering from pneumonia at mercy hospital.
     A   B   C   D
31 _____

32 Several universities of the south have excellent football teams.
     A   B   C
32 _____

33 The elm trees in sterling county were damaged by dutch elm disease.
   A   B   C   D   E
33 _____

34 The officer of the Michigan state police was praised by judge Marini
   A   B   C   D
   for his courage.
      E
34 _____

35 Our chorus sang "Joy to the world" at the christmas assembly.
    A   B   C
35 _____

36 I want my dad to meet your grandfather and your uncle Frank.
        A   B   C
36 _____

37 The ohio river is one of many rivers that flow into the mississippi.
    A B   C   D
37 _____

38 The Christy baking company on Park street makes
            A   B   C
   Dutch maid bread and cakes.
    D   E   F
38 _____

39 The zinnias bloom in august, but the asters don't bloom until fall.
    A   B   C   D
39 _____

40 The Rotary club meets every tuesday noon at the Banning hotel.
      A   B   C   D
40 _____

NAME_____ DATE_____ CLASS_____

UNIT 10-B HOW TO USE CAPITALS

Suppose that each of the following phrases occurred within a sentence. Write the letter of the <u>one</u> phrase in each group that is <u>correctly</u> printed.   [2 points each]

1 a. a Mexican Holiday   b. a Mexican holiday   c. a mexican Holiday   1 _____
2 a. the Chrysler building   b. the Chrysler Building   c. the chrysler building   2 _____
3 a. the author of this Poem   b. the Author of this poem
                c. the author of this poem   3 _____
4 a. a new high school   b. a new High School   c. a new High school   4 _____
5 a. on friday morning   b. on Friday Morning   c. on Friday morning   5 _____
6 a. to Sibley State Park   b. to Sibley state park   c. to Sibley State park   6 _____
7 a. with krunchie cornflakes   b. with Krunchie cornflakes
                c. with Krunchie Cornflakes   7 _____
8 a. in my History Class   b. in my History class   c. in my history class   8 _____
9 a. her new Chevrolet Convertible   b. her new chevrolet convertible
                c. her new Chevrolet convertible   9 _____
10 a. the new spring fashions   b. the new Spring fashions
                c. the new Spring Fashions   10 _____
11 a. with Italian Spaghetti   b. with Italian spaghetti
                c. with italian spaghetti   11 _____
12 a. the Waverly Theater   b. the Waverly theater   c. the waverly theater   12 _____
13 a. in our Literature book   b. in our literature book
                c. in our Literature Book   13 _____
14 a. read *The Call Of The Wild*   b. read *The call of the wild*
                c. read *The Call of the Wild*   14 _____
15 a. in all Catholic churches   b. in all Catholic Churches
                c. in all catholic churches   15 _____
16 a. to the Glenwood High School   b. to the Glenwood high school
                c. to the Glenwood High school   16 _____
17 a. any Hospital for children   b. any Hospital for Children
                c. any hospital for children   17 _____
18 a. for the Union oil company   b. for the Union Oil Company
                c. for the union oil company   18 _____
19 a. at the Ardmore Methodist Church   b. at the Ardmore Methodist church
                c. at the Ardmore methodist church   19 _____
20 a. with my Uncle and two Cousins   b. with my Uncle and two cousins
                c. with my uncle and two cousins   20 _____

Tests for English 2600

Copy with a small letter the one word in each line that should not be capitalized. [2 points each]

21	Hanukkah	Autumn	Baptist	21 _____
22	Appendicitis	Black	Harvard	22 _____
23	English	Clarinet	Brazil	23 _____
24	Bible	Latin II	Algebra	24 _____
25	Lawyer	Indian	American	25 _____
26	Europe	Cadillac	Baseball	26 _____
27	Broadway	Sparrow	Irish	27 _____
28	Collie	Halloween	February	28 _____
29	Wheaties	Chop Suey	Atlantic	29 _____
30	Christian	Spanish	Orchid	30 _____

Write the letter of each word that should be capitalized. [4 points for each sentence]

31 My father served french toast with strawberry jam for breakfast. 31 _____
      A   B   C   D

32 Several clubs of our high school will have a fall picnic at Rainbow park. 32 _____
      A   B   C   D

33 I forgot that thanksgiving comes on the fourth thursday in november. 33 _____
           A   B   C

34 I accompanied my uncle when he played his violin solo at a Methodist church
    A   B   C
   on Oakland avenue. 34 _____
            D

35 Norma, who was graduated from Harding business college, is assistant to the
                                      A   B
   director of the Armstrong steel company. 35 _____
       C   D   E

36 Our minister's wife bought the new easyday camera that was advertised in
    A   B   C
   last month's issue of *Woman's day*. 36 _____
      D   E

37 The men who signed the Declaration of independence would have been con-
                                           A
   sidered traitors if the american revolution had failed. 37 _____
                    B   C

38 My aunt took grandmother Brooks to visit her brother in oregon. 38 _____
    A   B   C   D

39 During Humanity week, a protestant and a catholic spoke on good will at
                 A   B   C
   our assembly. 39 _____
       D

40 All students read *A tale of two cities* in *literature* II. 40 _____
                A B C   D   E

NAME_____ DATE_____ CLASS_____

UNIT 11-A LEARNING TO USE COMMAS

Write the letter of the sentence that is <u>correctly</u> punctuated.   [4 points each]

1. a. A string broke in the middle of his selection but, the violinist continued to play.
   b. A string broke in the middle of his selection, but the violinist continued to play.   1 _____
2. a. Archie fell out of bed and didn't even wake up.
   b. Archie fell out of bed, and didn't even wake up.   2 _____
3. a. The band was playing "Anchors Aweigh" as we left the school auditorium.
   b. The band was playing, "Anchors Aweigh," as we left the school auditorium.   3 _____
4. a. The children of course, did not refuse the cake, and ice cream.
   b. The children, of course, did not refuse the cake and ice cream.   4 _____
5. a. Skyscrapers, railroads, bridges, and automobiles require large amounts of steel.
   b. Skyscrapers, railroads, bridges, and automobiles, require large amounts of steel.   5 _____
6. a. The car was found in front of a store at 2400 Jackson Avenue, Tulsa, Oklahoma.
   b. The car was found in front of a store at, 2400 Jackson Avenue, Tulsa Oklahoma.   6 _____
7. a. If you have forgotten Herb's birthday is next Tuesday.
   b. If you have forgotten, Herb's birthday is next Tuesday.   7 _____
8. a. Uncle Ben, my mother's brother in Connecticut, breeds and trains racehorses.
   b. Uncle Ben my mother's brother in Connecticut, breeds and trains racehorses.   8 _____
9. a. The sandwiches, and the cookies, and the lemonade disappeared within a few minutes.
   b. The sandwiches and the cookies and the lemonade disappeared within a few minutes.   9 _____
10. a. A clerk should not visit, or straighten out stock, while a customer is waiting to be served.
    b. A clerk should not visit or straighten out stock while a customer is waiting to be served.   10 _____
11. a. You'll be feeling fine, old friend, in just a few more days.
    b. You'll be feeling fine old friend, in just a few more days.   11 _____
12. a. When you hear the thunder you are safe from the lightning.
    b. When you hear the thunder, you are safe from the lightning.   12 _____

Tests for English 2600

Write the letters to indicate the points at which the commas should be omitted. [4 points for each sentence]

13 Mr. Turner, for example, saves time by not ironing shirts, or bath towels.   13 _____
          A   B   C

14 Walking home from school, Bobby made friends with a stray cat, and brought
                              A   B

    it home, with him.   14 _____
               C

15 After we finish Shakespeare's, *Julius Caesar,* our English class will
                                   A   B

    read, *David Copperfield.*   15 _____
           C

16 Louis, Stan, and I, were waiting for Gail, and Donna.   16 _____
          A   B   C

17 The records showed that on April 7, 1968, the store at, 1845 Westwood Avenue,
                                        A   B   C   D

    was sold to Ms. T. N. Stevens, the owner of several drugstores.   17 _____
                                   E

18 Chick slipped out, and ran away, when Martha, my young
                           A   B   C

    sister, opened the door.   18 _____
         D

19 The pitcher, and the catcher went into a huddle, and decided to pass Rowley,
                A   B   C

    the next batter.   19 _____

The following sentences are correct as they are printed. If you added the words in parentheses at the point indicated by the caret (∧), would one or more commas be necessary? Write *Yes* or *No* in the space at the right. [4 points each]

20 Frank cut and raked ∧ the lawn. (*and watered*)   20 _____
21 The driver was badly injured but ∧ is expected to live. (*he*)   21 _____
22 You must admit ∧ that you were partly to blame. (*of course*)   22 _____
23 Shep is a large dog ∧ . (*and requires a large amount of food*)   23 _____
24 The high mountains ∧ make the construction of roads very difficult. (*and the dense forests*)   24 _____
25 I complained to Mr. Foster ∧ about the slow service. (*the manager of the garage*)   25 _____

NAME_____ DATE_____ CLASS_____

UNIT 11-B LEARNING TO USE COMMAS

Write the letter of the sentence that is <u>correctly</u> punctuated. [4 points each]

1. a. It seems to me that only one other team, the New York Giants, ever did as well.
   b. It seems to me that only one other team, the New York Giants ever did as well. 1 _____

2. a. Sitting down on a log I took off my shoes, and shook out the sand and the pebbles.
   b. Sitting down on a log, I took off my shoes and shook out the sand and the pebbles. 2 _____

3. a. Paul earned money for his trip by washing cars, shoveling snow, and mowing lawns, for the neighbors.
   b. Paul earned money for his trip by washing cars, shoveling snow, and mowing lawns for the neighbors. 3 _____

4. a. Linda's parents approved of the plan, but I was doubtful.
   b. Linda's parents approved of the plan but, I was doubtful. 4 _____

5. a. One seaweed for example, may reach 600 feet in length.
   b. One seaweed, for example, may reach 600 feet in length. 5 _____

6. a. The city will have to increase the fares, or reduce the service.
   b. The city will have to increase the fares or reduce the service. 6 _____

7. a. If you can plan to visit me in July, or August.
   b. If you can, plan to visit me in July or August. 7 _____

8. a. It is little wonder that the child felt bitter and angry and lonely.
   b. It is little wonder that the child felt bitter, and angry, and lonely. 8 _____

9. a. The defense proved that Chandler was in Atlanta, Georgia, on the night of March 11, 1968.
   b. The defense proved that Chandler was in, Atlanta, Georgia, on the night of, March 11, 1968. 9 _____

10. a. I have decided my friend, to take your advice.
    b. I have decided, my friend, to take your advice. 10 _____

11. a. After reading Jesse Stuart's "The Split Cherry Tree," I decided to adapt it for a radio script.
    b. After reading Jesse Stuart's, "The Split Cherry Tree," I decided to adapt it for a radio script. 11 _____

12. a. You can decide whether to stop, or to continue, after you have taken a few dancing lessons.
    b. You can decide whether to stop or to continue after you have taken a few dancing lessons. 12 _____

Tests for English 2600

Write the letters to indicate the points at which the commas should be omitted. [4 points for each sentence]

13 Mother packed us some fruit, and sandwiches, and we started for the beach.   13 _____
            A   B

14 No, I'm quite sure that none of us cares to discuss the matter
     A
    with Loren, while he is in his present mood.   14 _____
              B

15 Calvin Coolidge, was the first President to address the nation, by radio.   15 _____
                   A   B

16 Cathy, one of my girl friends, lost control of her skates, and
        A   B   C
    crashed into a full-length mirror, cutting both her hands.   16 _____
                                     D

17 Your sister, I suppose, will become a lawyer, or a doctor.   17 _____
               A   B   C

18 Our records show, that the check was mailed to Phoenix, Arizona,
                    A   B   C
    on, May 12, 1961.   18 _____
      D   E

19 Ever since I was a small child, bugs, worms, and snakes, have frightened me.   19 _____
                                  A   B   C   D

The following sentences are correct as they are printed. If you added the words in parentheses at the point indicated by the caret (∧), would one or more commas be necessary? Write *Yes* or *No* in the space at the right.   [4 points each]

20 Luther Burbank ∧ developed many new flowers and vegetables. (*a great botanist*)   20 _____

21 The ice ∧ was too soft for skating. (*however*)   21 _____

22 Many friends ∧ contributed generously to the fund. (*and neighbors*)   22 _____

23 How can Wally study and eat ∧ at the same time? (*and listen to the radio*)   23 _____

24 I was washing clothes in the basement ∧ . (*and didn't hear the doorbell*)   24 _____

25 Mr. Krantz turned around and ∧ looked at us disapprovingly. (*he*)   25 _____

NAME_____ DATE_____ CLASS_____

UNIT 12-A APOSTROPHES AND QUOTATION MARKS

Write the letter of the sentence that does <u>not</u> have an error in the use of apostrophes.   [3 points each]

1. a. The childs' operation used up most of his parents' savings.
   b. The child's operation used up most of his parents' savings.
   c. The childs' operation used up most of his parent's savings.   1 _____

2. a. Several student's ideas of its meaning were different from Tom's.
   b. Several students' ideas of its meaning were different from Tom's.
   c. Several students' ideas of it's meaning were different from Toms.   2 _____

3. a. Carol's flute is just like hers except that it's lighter.
   b. Carol's flute is just like her's except that it's lighter.
   c. Carols' flute is just like hers except that its lighter.   3 _____

4. a. The sale includes womens' dresses and men's suits.
   b. The sale includes women's dresses and mens' suits.
   c. The sale includes women's dresses and men's suits.   4 _____

5. a. This newspaper's plan was to print as many voter's opinions as possible before the election.
   b. This newspaper's plan was to print as many voters' opinions as possible before the election.
   c. This newspapers' plan was to print as many voters' opinions as possible before the election.   5 _____

6. a. The childrens' toys were scattered all over the Bradys' lawn.
   b. The children's toys were scattered all over the Brady's lawn.
   c. The children's toys were scattered all over the Bradys' lawn.   6 _____

7. a. Why should the boys expect two days' pay for one day's work?
   b. Why should the boys' expect two days' pay for one days' work?
   c. Why should the boys expect two day's pay for one day's work?   7 _____

8. a. The women's committee studied each candidate's record before making its recommendation.
   b. The women's committee studied each candidates' record before making its recommendation.
   c. The womens' committee studied each candidate's record before making its recommendation.   8 _____

9. a. The teacher could'nt read several pupils' papers.
   b. The teacher couldn't read several pupils' papers.
   c. The teacher couldn't read several pupil's papers.   9 _____

10. a. Harold's voice could be heard above the other boy's voices.
    b. Harolds' voice could be heard above the other boys' voices.
    c. Harold's voice could be heard above the other boys' voices.   10 _____

Tests for English 2600

Write the letter of the sentence in which the contractions are spelled correctly. [2 points each]

11 a. We're sure it is'nt so.   b. We're sure it isn't so.   c. Were sure it isn't so.   11 _____
12 a. He doesnt know who's going.   b. He does'nt know who'se going.
    c. He doesn't know who's going.   12 _____
13 a. Let's see if they're ripe.   b. Lets see if they're ripe.
    c. Let's see if their ripe.   13 _____
14 a. Arn't you glad you'r wrong?   b. Aren't you glad you're wrong?
    c. Are'nt you glad you're wrong?   14 _____

Copy the correct word in each pair. [3 points for each sentence]

15 We must try to save (*its, it's*) life before (*its, it's*) too late.   15 _____ _____
16 (*You're, Your*) leaving without (*your, you're*) ticket.   16 _____ _____
17 (*Whose, Who's*) the one (*whose, who's*) name was called?   17 _____ _____
18 If (*their, they're*) home, (*they're, their*) lights will be on.   18 _____ _____
19 (*It's, Its*) trying to escape from (*it's, its*) cage.   19 _____ _____
20 (*Their, They're*) sure that (*your, you're*) going to succeed.   20 _____ _____
21 (*Whose, Who's*) the boy that (*you're, your*) inviting?   21 _____ _____
22 (*Whose, Who's*) car is in front of (*they're, their*) house?   22 _____ _____

Each sentence contains one or more words from which the apostrophe should be omitted. Copy these words, omitting the apostrophes. [2 points for each sentence]

23 The Kohlers' boat isn't as fast as our's.   23 _____ _____
24 Picking the pear's was a full day's work.   24 _____ _____
25 Let's find out if the Judd's want to sell their's.   25 _____ _____
26 Melvin get's his stamp's from his father's collection.   26 _____ _____
27 The dance's are held in the boys' gym on Friday night's.   27 _____ _____

Write the letter of the sentence which is correctly punctuated. [4 points each]

28 a. "It was like shooting fish in a barrel," laughed the coach.
    b. "It was like shooting fish in a barrel, laughed the coach."   28 _____
29 a. The customer complained, "That the steak was tough."
    b. The customer complained that the steak was tough.   29 _____
30 a. "You can't swim here," said the lifeguard.
    b. "You can't swim here", said the lifeguard.   30 _____
31 a. "Is your mother at home?," asked the agent.
    b. "Is your mother at home?" asked the agent.   31 _____
32 a. "Why won't this car start," questioned Pete?
    b. "Why won't this car start?" questioned Pete.   32 _____
33 a. Mrs. Dawson replied, "You can't take it with you."
    b. Mrs. Dawson replied "You can't take it with you".   33 _____
34 a. "What a complete waste of money," exclaimed my sister!
    b. "What a complete waste of money!" exclaimed my sister.   34 _____

NAME_____ DATE_____ CLASS_____

UNIT 12-B APOSTROPHES AND QUOTATION MARKS

Write the letter of the sentence that does <u>not</u> have an error in the use of apostrophes.   [3 points each]

1 a. My friend's trouble is that he will take no ones' advice.
   b. My friends' trouble is that he will take no one's advice.
   c. My friend's trouble is that he will take no one's advice.   **1** _____

2 a. There's a vacant lot between the Crosbys' house and ours.
   b. There's a vacant lot between the Crosbys' house and our's.
   c. Theres a vacant lot between the Crosby's house and ours.   **2** _____

3 a. Womens' fashions change more often than men's fashions.
   b. Women's fashions change more often than mens' fashions.
   c. Women's fashions change more often than men's fashions.   **3** _____

4 a. The treasurers' job is to collect all the member's dues.
   b. The treasurer's job is to collect all the members' dues.
   c. The treasurer's job is to collect all the members due's.   **4** _____

5 a. The judge's opinion was that the accident was due to both drivers' carelessness.
   b. The judge's opinion was that the accident was due to both driver's carelessness.
   c. The judges' opinion was that the accident was due to both driver's carelessness.   **5** _____

6 a. All the winner's pictures will be in Sunday's paper.
   b. All the winners' pictures will be in Sunday's paper.
   c. All the winners' pictures will be in Sundays' paper.   **6** _____

7 a. The man's appearance aroused both officer's suspicions.
   b. The mans' appearance aroused both officers' suspicions.
   c. The man's appearance aroused both officers' suspicions.   **7** _____

8 a. The girls' games are as well attended as the boy's.
   b. The girls' games are as well attended as the boys'.
   c. The girl's games are as well attended as the boys'.   **8** _____

9 a. The speaker's remarks hurt some people's feelings.
   b. The speakers' remarks hurt some peoples' feelings.
   c. The speaker's remarks hurt some peoples' feelings.   **9** _____

10 a. You should have seen the childrens' faces after the principal's announcement.
   b. You should have seen the children's faces after the principals' announcement.
   c. You should have seen the children's faces after the principal's announcement.   **10** _____

Write the letter of the sentence in which the contractions are spelled correctly. [2 points each]

11 a. Let's see who's here.   b. Let's see who'se here.   c. Lets see who's here.   11 _____

12 a. We're sure that he does'nt know.   b. Were sure that he doesn't know.
      c. We're sure that he doesn't know.   12 _____

13 a. Your afraid that it isn't right.   b. You're afraid that it isn't right.
      c. You're afraid that it isent right.   13 _____

14 a. They're sorry you arn't going.   b. Their sorry you aren't going.
      c. They're sorry you aren't going.   14 _____

Copy the correct word in each pair. [3 points for each sentence]

15 (*Its, It's*) nose should be cold if (*its, it's*) healthy.   15 _____ _____
16 (*You're, Your*) expected to do (*your, you're*) share.   16 _____ _____
17 (*Who's Whose*) instrument is not in (*its, it's*) case?   17 _____ _____
18 (*Their, They're*) standing in line for (*they're, their*) tickets.   18 _____ _____
19 (*It's, Its*) looking for (*it's, its*) mother.   19 _____ _____
20 (*Whose, Who's*) paying (*their, they're*) bus fare?   20 _____ _____
21 (*Their, They're*) sure (*your, you're*) not serious.   21 _____ _____
22 (*Who's, Whose*) the player (*whose, who's*) batting for Fisher?   22 _____ _____

Each sentence contains one or more words from which the apostrophe should be omitted. Copy these words, omitting the apostrophes. [2 points for each sentence]

23 The Hills' farm is an hour's drive from Niagara Fall's.   23 _____ _____
24 Their score's are better than Central's.   24 _____ _____
25 Let's see if the Colburn's will let us use their's.   25 _____ _____
26 Joyce made her's with ten cents' worth of pipe cleaner's.   26 _____ _____
27 She get's a week's vacation at the company's expense.   27 _____ _____

Write the letter of the sentence which is correctly punctuated. [4 points each]

28 a. The mechanic said, "That the car needed a new muffler."
    b. The mechanic said that the car needed a new muffler.   28 _____

29 a. The little girl replied, "My name is Mary Ann."
    b. The little girl replied my name is Mary Ann.   29 _____

30 a. "Isn't Floyd ready yet?" asked Bob impatiently.
    b. "Isn't Floyd ready yet?," asked Bob impatiently.   30 _____

31 a. "The picture has just started", said the usher.
    b. "The picture has just started," said the usher.   31 _____

32 a. "Have you ever seen a better fit?" asked the salesperson.
    b. "Have you ever seen a better fit," asked the salesperson?   32 _____

33 a. The little boy replied regretfully "My mommy won't let me".
    b. The little boy replied regretfully, "My mommy won't let me."   33 _____

34 a. "What a huge pumpkin," exclaimed Uncle Oscar!
    b. "What a huge pumpkin!" exclaimed Uncle Oscar.   34 _____

NAME_____ DATE_____ CLASS_____

FINAL TEST

After each statement write *True* or *False* in the space at the right. [1 point each]

1 A verb can consist of more than one word. 1 _____
2 Any verb can take either a direct object or a subject complement. 2 _____
3 An adjective can modify a verb. 3 _____
4 An adverb can modify an adjective or another adverb. 4 _____
5 A prepositional phrase could consist of only two words. 5 _____
6 Every prepositional phrase contains a subject and a verb. 6 _____
7 Two sentences joined by *and*, *but*, or *or* would be a compound sentence. 7 _____
8 A clause beginning with *when*, *because*, *if*, or *although* would generally be an adverb clause. 8 _____
9 An adjective clause is one that modifies an adjective. 9 _____
10 A sentence with an adverb or adjective clause is a compound sentence. 10 _____

Indicate the pattern of each sentence by writing one of the following letters: [2 points each]

      A = Subject — Verb
      B = Subject — Verb → Direct Object
      C = Subject — Linking Verb ← Subject Complement

11 Her partner was silent during the dance. 11 _____
12 The speaker of the committee resigned. 12 _____
13 The Roman Colosseum is the world's largest ruin. 13 _____
14 Evelyn's intelligence impressed the manager. 14 _____
15 The milk in our refrigerator froze. 15 _____

Eliminate the *and* by changing the italicized statement to the kind of word group indicated in the parentheses. Rewrite each sentence. [3 points each]

16 *Pete reached the light*, and he turned in the wrong direction. (adverb clause) _____
_____

17 We had a large map, and *it showed all the state parks*. (adjective clause) _____
_____

18 *The novel is long*, and it is very interesting. (adverb clause) _____
_____

19 *Mother smelled burnt food*, and she rushed to the kitchen. (*-ing* word group) _____
_____

Tests for English 2600

20 Ruth West played a solo, and *she is a talented young pianist.* (appositive) _____

Identify each word group, using the following letters: [1 point each]

F = Fragment   S = Sentence   R S = Run-on Sentence

21 Thinking that I could change my mind later.   21 _____
22 The lake is stony, it hurts one's feet.   22 _____
23 While she was attending school, Wanda worked for a druggist during the evenings and on Saturdays.   23 _____
24 One brother went to the city, the other remained on the farm.   24 _____
25 A good driver looks ahead at least one hundred yards, the length of a football field.   25 _____
26 Which caused me to change my mind about school.   26 _____

Copy the correct word in each pair. [1 point each]

27 I (*saw, seen*) Helen at church this morning.   27 _____
28 Several store windows were (*broke, broken*) by the wind during last night's storm.   28 _____
29 The Sandovals must have (*gone, went*) to their cottage.   29 _____
30 Matt must have (*driven, drove*) down the wrong road.   30 _____
31 Rosa (*come, came*) home from college yesterday.   31 _____
32 I should have (*took, taken*) my raincoat along.   32 _____
33 This morning I (*ran, run*) into an old friend.   33 _____
34 Why don't you (*lie, lay*) down and rest for a while?   34 _____
35 She had just (*lain, laid*) her purse on the counter for a minute.   35 _____
36 Steve never (*lets, leaves*) anything interfere with his work.   36 _____
37 The appearance of one's clothes (*tells, tell*) something about one.   37 _____
38 This style (*don't, doesn't*) cost any more than the other.   38 _____
39 One of my cousins (*play, plays*) professional football.   39 _____
40 There (*was, were*) a pile of dishes on the kitchen sink.   40 _____
41 The theft of these papers (*create, creates*) a serious problem.   41 _____
42 A doctor or a nurse (*are, is*) always in attendance.   42 _____
43 Any outbursts of temper (*was, were*) not tolerated.   43 _____
44 He was much too sleepy to drive (*an, a*) automobile.   44 _____
45 Our family didn't go (*nowhere, anywhere*) last summer.   45 _____
46 The garage fixed the fender very (*satisfactory, satisfactorily*).   46 _____
47 Grace looks (*beautiful, beautifully*) in her new red dress.   47 _____
48 I can't paint (*well, good*) with this old brush.   48 _____
49 The new market sells good meat quite (*reasonable, reasonably*).   49 _____
50 No teacher could be (*friendlier, more friendlier*) than Ms. Trombley.   50 _____
51 The Harts and (*we, us*) shared the cost of the fence.   51 _____

NAME_____ DATE_____ CLASS_____

FINAL TEST   (Continued)

52 This game will break the tie between the Rangers and (*they, them*). **52** _____
53 The coach asked Ken and (*I, me*) to take tickets at the game. **53** _____
54 Roy doesn't study as much as (*her, she*). **54** _____
55 Mr. Sanders offered the use of his boat to (*we, us*) students. **55** _____
56 The school helps handicapped people to help (*themselves, theirselves*). **56** _____
57 I'm not certain that (*they're, their*) coming. **57** _____
58 We don't know yet (*who's, whose*) car it was. **58** _____
59 I (*couldn't, could*) hardly see the number on the house. **59** _____

Write the letter of the sentence in which capitals are used <u>correctly</u>.   [2 points each]

60 a. My father considers Coach Wyman one of the best football coaches in the state.
   b. My Father considers Coach Wyman one of the best Football coaches in the state.
   c. My father considers coach Wyman one of the best football coaches in the State.   **60** _____

61 a. The new hotel near Prospect park was designed by a famous Architect.
   b. The new hotel near Prospect Park was designed by a famous architect.
   c. The new Hotel near Prospect Park was designed by a famous architect.   **61** _____

62 a. "Joy To The World," a popular Christmas carol, is based on music by Handel, a German composer.
   b. "Joy to the World," a popular Christmas carol, is based on music by Handel, a German composer.
   c. "Joy to the World," a popular christmas carol, is based on music by Handel, a german composer.   **62** _____

Write the letter of the sentence that does <u>not</u> have an error in the use of apostrophes.   [2 points each]

63 a. The childrens' room is right next to ours.
   b. The children's room is right next to our's.
   c. The children's room is right next to ours.   **63** _____

64 a. It's this store's policy to check other stores' prices.
   b. It's this store's policy to check other store's prices.
   c. Its this store's policy to check other stores' prices.   **64** _____

65 a. Several speakers voice's couldn't be heard in the balcony.
   b. Several speakers' voices couldn't be heard in the balcony.
   c. Several speaker's voices could'nt be heard in the balcony.   **65** _____

Write the letter of the sentence which is correctly punctuated. [2 points each]

66 a. The Pattons our next-door neighbors, sold their home and moved to a farm.
    b. The Pattons, our next-door neighbors, sold their home and moved to a farm.
    c. The Pattons, our next-door neighbors, sold their home, and moved to a farm. 66 _____

67 a. We shall be at the Rainbow Hotel, 622 Forest Avenue until Friday July 29.
    b. We shall be at the Rainbow Hotel 622 Forest Avenue until, Friday, July 29.
    c. We shall be at the Rainbow Hotel, 622 Forest Avenue, until Friday, July 29. 67 _____

68 a. Colfax, and Glenwood High are in the same county, and the rivalry between them is very great.
    b. Colfax and Glenwood High, are in the same county and the rivalry between them is very great.
    c. Colfax and Glenwood High are in the same county, and the rivalry between them is very great. 68 _____

69 a. This legislation, by the way, is important to every man, woman, and child in the nation.
    b. This legislation by the way, is important to every man, woman, and child in the nation.
    c. This legislation, by the way, is important to every man, woman, and child, in the nation. 69 _____

70 a. Expecting some important company, we tidied up our yard, after we had given our house a thorough cleaning.
    b. Expecting some important company, we tidied up our yard after we had given our house a thorough cleaning.
    c. Expecting some important company we tidied up our yard, after we had given our house a thorough cleaning. 70 _____

71 a. The coach replied, "We can't win every game."
    b. The coach replied "We can't win every game."
    c. The coach replied, "We can't win every game". 71 _____

72 a. "When do we start? asked Bob."
    b. "When do we start," asked Bob?
    c. "When do we start?" asked Bob. 72 _____